Owen
Wister's
West

OWEN WISTER'S WEST

∿∿∿

Selected Articles

Edited by Robert Murray Davis

University of New Mexico Press

Albuquerque

Library of Congress Cataloging-in-Publication Data

Wister, Owen, 1860–1938.
Owen Wister's West.

Bibliography: p.
Contents: Introduction—The white goat and his
country—The evolution of the cow-puncher [etc.]
1. Wister, Owen, 1860–1938—Journeys—West (U.S.)
2. Authors, American—19th century—Journeys—West (U.S.)
3. West (U.S.)—Description and travel—1880–1950.
I. Davis, Robert Murray.   I. Title.
PS3346.A34   1987   814'.52   87-9218
ISBN 0-8263-0994-1
ISBN 0-8263-1005-2 (pbk.)

For Jeanette Gregory Harris

Contents

Acknowledgments

The staffs of the Southwestern Collection at Texas Tech University and of the Western History Collection at the University of Oklahoma assisted me in finding materials which patrons and directors have had the vision to gather. The Proposal Services office of the University of Oklahoma, under the direction of Dr. Kenneth Hoving, vice-provost for Research Administration, provided copying service. Megan Davis served as research assistant and fairly adequate daughter. Ray Merlock offered advice, encouragement, and bibliographical material. Had it not been for Jeanette Gregory Harris, the project would never have gotten started.

Owen
Wister's
West

Introduction

As the neurasthenic young man traveled toward Wyoming in the company of two middle-aged spinsters (who was escorting whom was not clearly defined), he saw the West from the perspective which his training had given him. The landscape, like *Die Walküre,* was "much more than my most romantic dream could have hoped," and the sudden appearance of horsemen and cattle was "like Genesis" (*Owen Wister Out West,* 30–31). Once settled at the ranch of Major Frank Wolcott, he felt relieved to put away his eastern habits of thought: "I'm beginning to be able to feel that I'm something of an animal and not a stinking brain alone. Nailed up a strip of cloth over the crack of the big dugout door to keep the flies from the meat" (32).

Mythic vision, physical and psychic renewal, and realistic perception—three different if not conflicting responses appear not only in Wister's first response to the West in 1885 but, together with an impulse to place the region and society historically, in most of his writing, fiction as well as non-fiction, about the West. The emphasis on rebirth through healing immersion of the hyperaesthetic, self-conscious dude in the splendors of the American West is not surprising: Wister articulated it in his writing and embodied it in his life so well that his case is almost archetypal. Certainly the few readers who know that Wister wrote *The Virginian* and the even fewer who know that he wrote anything else see him in this pattern.

There is ample reason to do so. Wister's heredity and training prepared him to be a very successful "stinking brain." An ancestor had signed the Constitution; his grandmother, Fanny Kemble, was a distinguished actress and author; his mother was clever enough to be interested in—and, even cleverer, to interest—Henry James; his father was a successful physician. Young Owen was precocious, reading and counting time to music at the age of four because of his mother's tutelage, unscrewing the bars on his window to climb out on the roof and screwing them back to escape detection because of his native wit. Home life was not perfect: his mother broke down after her father's death—short and long-term memory were impaired—and his father worked so hard that he made rounds between his mother's death and funeral—and next day could not even write a prescription. Dr. Wister's three-year recuperation in Europe took his son to a series of hotels, rather like a genteel version of Randolph in James's *Daisy Miller,* and to schools in Switzerland and England, where he learned more about music and nature. When the family returned to America, he went first to St. Paul's preparatory school, where he felt the need to go camping so as not "to be a 'house-boy' " (Payne, 24), and then to Harvard. In Cambridge, he was a brilliant social and academic success: all the right clubs and all the right friends; writing and composing for undergraduate magazines and musicals; and a *summa cum laude* in music and philosophy despite his parents' fear that he would not graduate.

Then he made a version of the Grand Tour, carrying a letter of introduction to Franz Liszt, who listened to one of his compositions, suggested a friendly revision, and announced to Fanny Kemble that the youth had *"un talent pronouncé* for music" (Wister, 22). In Paris, his teachers felt the same way, but Dr. Wister's experience with artists *manqué* in Rome combined with his Quaker background and class prejudices ("Liszt is a damn Jew, and I am an American gentleman," he wrote of the composer's praise of his son [*That I May,* 112]) to make him insist that Owen should either have genius as a composer or be mediocre at a more settled profession. But he abandoned his opposition to music—and received his son's capitulation in which he forsook music to enter a business career in a letter full of well-bred agonies of self-doubt.

Established in a Boston bank, young Wister turned to the

company of the Tavern Club and to writing a *Bildungsroman* which William Dean Howells thought too gamey for an American to publish. Denied this outlet, Wister found the only relief which his family pattern allowed: he fell ill. The trip to Wyoming, prescribed by relative-physician-novelist Weir Mitchell, gave Wister the energy to go to law school. More active expeditions in 1887, 1888 (when he guided cowboys and Indians through the mountains), and 1889 got him through it and into a Philadelphia law firm. He denied rather sardonically to his father that he planned to settle in the West.

The West had healed him, but while physical and spiritual regeneration were important to him, Americans seem incapable of simply being; they have to do something. Even as Wister congratulated himself in July 1885 on being more than "a stinking brain," that brain was prompting him a week later

> to find out all about [the West]—and master it—theoretically. It's a life as strange as any the country has seen, and it will slowly make way for Cheyennes, Chicagos, and ultimately inland New Yorks— everything reduced to the same flat prairie-like level of utilitarian civilization. Branans and Beeches will give way to Tweeds and Jay Gould—and the ticker will replace the rifle (*Owen Wister Out West*, 35).

Yet he was ambivalent about both East and West and never quite certain of what role he could play. For a while, the West offered him an exhilarating multiplicity of roles in which he felt free from socially imposed restraints. At the end of his second trip West—during which he had killed his first bear—he noted that he had been mistaken for an Englishman, a drummer, a bartender, and a stage driver and concluded rather sadly that "in another day or so I shall be back where nobody takes me for anyone but myself, and my period of entertainment will have ceased for a long while" (61). The West was the ideal place for role-shifting: even the houses of Gardiner, Montana, "resemble theatre scenery for a sensational drama" (61). Besides, as he wrote to his mother, "You would die in a moment" in Buffalo, Wyoming, not so much because of the land but because of the people—"Not," as I have heard a modern Philadelphian put it, "our class, dear!" (116) Writing to keep an accurate record rather than to fend off his mother, he admitted that Buffalo was not all that bad. In an even more daring moment, he boasted to his mother that "this United States is an irrepressible country. I have heard many things, all of them in some superlative degree [so] funny or horrible that my terms of thought and standard of measure are entirely changed" (192).

This is the same spirit that earlier had led him to climb out on the roof and to write to his mother about social and physical trials too difficult for her. He sometimes sounds like Tom Sawyer on a carefully limited spree: he always screwed the bars back in, and he always came back to Philadelphia.

But it would be a mistake, or at least an exaggeration, to identify Wister with Tom. For one thing, the Philadelphian had a real appreciation of style as an internal structure, not just as external panache. For another, he never got so caught up in his fantasies that he tried to play a role, as Westerner or anything else, in which he did not really belong. Thus he refused to wear chaps until Dean Duke, a cowboy who resembled the character of the Virginian that was forming in Wister's mind, gave him a pair. And unlike Tom, he had read not just Scott and Dumas and other romancers but Howells and James—and Mark Twain. Therefore, while he rejoiced that the country and people kept his mother at bay and always surrendered to "this glorious, this supernatural atmosphere . . . better, clearer, more magical than ever I remembered it" (98), he could also see that the country was like "a face without eyebrows" (99) and "that life in this negligent irresponsible wilderness turns people shiftless, cruel, and incompetent" and could judge as severely as any of his Quaker ancestors "a sloth in doing anything and everything, that is born of the deceitful ease with which makeshifts answer here." This new judgment was prompted by his reaction to the gouging of a horse's eye (the story version disturbed Theodore Roosevelt so badly that, in deference to his wishes, Wister cut it out of *The Virginian*), and it occasioned, if not gave rise to, epic ambitions:

Did I believe in the efficacy of prayer, I should petition to be the hand that once for all chronicled and laid bare the virtues and the vices of this extraordinary phase of American social progress. Nobody has done it. Nobody has touched anywhere near it. A few have described external sights and incidents, but the grand total thing—its rise, its hysterical unreal prosperity, and its disenchanting downfall. All this and its influence on the various sorts of human character that has been subjected to it has not been hinted at by a single writer that I, at least, have heard of (112–13).

By the time he wrote this passage in 1891, he had more than an inkling of what, he said in a letter to his mother the next day, he would do with his observations: "write a great fat book about the whole thing" (114). He observed and recorded diligently. Besides details of equipment and movement, he recorded the talk of all kinds of men, finding the most flavor in that of Henry Smith, an authentic bad man whom Wister contrasted with literary villains.

Amid this whirl of sensations and language, he wrote to his mother that his descriptions of the West "must be Hebrew to you" (128). But if he was going to render the material, he would have to translate it, render it, for his mother and other easterners. "The light that never was on land or sea" made him "wish I could draw. Writing is so wretched" (103). He always had a keen sense of the painter's art: later he rejoiced at having Remington's illustrations for his work; always he maintained something of the painterly eye. For landscape, it was more often the eye of Albert Bierstadt or Thomas Moran than that of Remington. But the foreground was seen with the eye of the realist. The high mountains could be "too damned cold for romance and nature," and the flies got at the meat which the animal in Wister was to consume. The air was glorious; the mountains were majestic; the towns were crude and slovenly; the population, puzzlingly mixed, seemed to come out of no past and to be going toward no clear future. And he knew that he would have to render it as a writer and a realist, asking himself, "Can I apply acid to my English, tell nothing till the sharp cutting metal is left?" (99).

As he told the story almost forty years after the event, he was dining in a Philadelphia club in the fall of 1891 and talking with Walter Furness about the West. Fortified by the wine, they asked each other:

> Why wasn't some Kipling saving the sage-brush for American litera-
> ture, before the sage-brush and all that it signified went the way of
> the California forty-niner, went the way of the Mississippi steam-
> boat, went the way of everything? Roosevelt had seen the sage-
> brush true, had felt its poetry; and also Remington, who illustrated
> his articles so well. But what was fiction doing, fiction, the only
> thing that has always outlived fact? Must it be perpetual tea-cups?
> Was Alkali Ike in the comic papers the one figure which the jejune
> American imagination, always at fullcock to banter or to brag,
> could discern in that epic which was being lived at a gallop out in the
> sage-brush? (Wister, 29).

Wister went from dining room to library and by midnight had written a substantial portion of "Hank's Woman," his first west-ern story. This makes a good story; but in the June–August journals of 1891, he is very much a writer recording material to be worked up and outlining projects to be realized. More important is the reference to Kipling, for like many of his contemporaries, he regarded Kipling as a realist. Wister's own literary credo asserted "that the whole of life is fiction's field, that nothing is wrong that hurts nobody, that within the very shifting limits of good taste anything can be told, and that the writer should leave moralizing to the reader" (16). More simply, as he put it in his diary, "I value accuracy more than any other quality"; even more simply, "I don't like to write about places that I have not been" (*Owen Wister Out West*, 223, 220).

His first two stories were published in 1892, another pair came out in 1893, and in the middle of that year he was invoking his muse, in very mediocre poetry, for inspiration of work that in-cluded stories and a major book about "The Course of Empire," perhaps an outgrowth of his epic ambitions of 1891. He seemed happy with the direction, if not the velocity, of his career, for writing about the West validated his earlier trips in a way that a search for health or recreation would not. Besides, more writing meant more trips.

But just before his thirty-third birthday (July 14, 1893), Henry Miles Alden of Harper & Brothers changed his literal as well as his literary direction, offering a contract for eight stories to be published in *Harper's Monthly* and then in volume form (*Red Men and White*, he finally called it, rejecting a suggestion by the real Kipling), illustrated by Frederic Remington. Alden was quite explicit:

> Each must be a thrilling story, having its ground in a real incident, though you are left free scope for imaginative treatment. Where possible . . . you will confine yourself to actuality. . . . We wish in this series to portray certain features of Western life which are now rapidly disappearing with the progress of civilization. Not the least striking of these is that of the appeal to lynch law, which ought to give capital subject for one of your stories (Payne, 138).

The pun in the final clause was perhaps intentional, but Wister took the suggestion lightly enough in writing "The Serenade at Siskiyou," in which criminals coddled by sentimental women are taken out and hanged by their sensible menfolk.

However, there were some differences between what Alden said and what Wister heard and between what Wister desired and what he was willing to do. At first it seemed simple:

> If I can write what is wanted of me, I shall certainly have eaten the cake and had it too. Alden wants me to do the whole adventure of the West in sketches or fiction, as I find most suitable in each case— taking Indian fighting, train robbery, what I please (*Owen Wister Out West,* 167).

But on almost immediate reflection, he could see some drawbacks to the proposition:

> Events in my literary life have crowded so thick of late that I am a little bewildered. . . . Alden wants my studies to pause for a while and says that after a series of pure adventure the studies will have a wider popularity. I insisted that I believed in my studies and had no

wish to be interrupted or discouraged in my road through them to
the final goal of "The Course of Empire," and he entirely assented to
the desirableness of the scheme, saying those other would merely
put in abeyance meanwhile [sic]. So now my next duty is to hunt
material of adventure voraciously (168).

The contract made him an instant success, but it took him
farther out of his way than he anticipated: to the Southwest rather
than to Wyoming; to the writing of romance rather than epic; to a
consideration of the West piecemeal rather than as a whole. "The
Course of Empire," nominally postponed, was never to be re-
sumed in anything like the same form. Lin McLean and the
Virginian, embodiments of the cowboy emerging from his imaginative encounter with the setting and people of Wyoming, could
not for the moment be developed. Even Wister's most successful
narrative method—the inexperienced but not quite foolish tenderfoot narrating, and giving a stylistic and contextual sophistica-
tion to, a story which is in part interpreted by a perceptive
westerner, could not be used for the *Harper's* stories because it
presented character rather than "pure adventure."

But he did not hesitate, and off he went. He did not like the
Southwest, "a forlorn, wretched place . . . . all right to write fire-
and-smoke romances [like "La Tinaja Bonita"] about, but there it
ends" (204). Some things pleased him: "the easy outdoor un-
ruffled days . . . spent in the company of people who feel as I do
about things in life" and "flattery, the real, delicious sort" (203).
But the arid mountains made him long for Wind River—"a
stream is surely the moving life that holds the source of mountain
charm"—(242) and on his second journey, he knew that the trips
to the Northwest "were holidays from the law and my perfunc-
tory days at the office—the forgetting for a moment of a detested
occupation. This made them delicious, and these Wind River days
with George West had an enchantment that no doubt can never be
wrought again" (201). By 1895 he began his last trip for *Harper's*,
reluctant to leave the East, and ended it with "Damn material-
hunting! I'm filled and sick with it. But the hand is on the plough
and must remain faithful" (250).

Having become a professional author, he had found—and been cast in—a role, and he sometimes felt anxious about that role. Returning to the scene of a story he had already written, he felt rather odd: "I had been writing a story about being there [Solomonville] for so many weeks before leaving home that the fiction was still somehow in my mind and made a comical jumble with the fact" (238). Even more oddly, connections he thought he had only imagined turned out to be true. And the need to gather material affected the ways in which he saw people and places—he was a reporter, almost a spy. When his first stories had appeared, he could enjoy, anonymously, the response to his tales of strangers encountered on trains. Now he was subjected to cross-examination about the Modoc War, which he had been investigating, by a General Schofield (244). He passed that quiz, but, still a gentleman, he never wrote about that war because the villain turned out to be the father of a woman who had been hospitable to him, and he would not let imagination or even civility tamper with the facts.

The *Harper's* series ended, the collection of stories assembled from it was a moderate critical success, and Wister turned back to Lin McLean and the Virginian and, advised and prodded by Remington, to "The Evolution of the Cow-Puncher," the only result of the plan for "The Course of Empire" (Vorpahl, 66–76). This essay was pivotal in Wister's career, but it was a different kind of pivot than he had anticipated. Up to this point, he had been primarily concerned with recording fresh experience of the West. From now on, details of description and sensation were drawn primarily from his early diaries. After and to some extent in "The Evolution," he was less concerned with the setting and the people than with what they meant.

Looked at closely, the essay is an odd mixture of reporting and romance, and its tone is an uneasy blend of history and nostalgia. Wister could see the immediate causes and effects of the end of the open range. Others saw much the same result: Frederic Jackson Turner, two years younger, gave his epoch-marking speech the same year that Wister received the *Harper's* contract. But Wister was not willing to give up the idea of the West. His only refuge from nostalgia was a kind of theory of atavism, in which strength and independence appropriate in the untamed lands of the West remained in the select few individuals and in the very best, mixed with aristocratic and chivalric values to produce those who would save America from sinking into a swarm of commercialized, urbanized mongrels.

Wister's racial and social prejudices were those of his class and period, but his expression of them was for a time tempered by his hope that the best qualities of the West could leaven the East. He had formed the plan for *The Virginian* by 1896, and at the turn of the century wrote four essays which provide an intellectual framework for the novel. In "Concerning Bad Men," Wister uses an anecdote (he never saw anything this wild) to show that bravery and resourcefulness are not by themselves sufficient for heroism. The young protagonist is a kind of fallen version of the Virginian—or for that matter of "Theodore Roosevelt: The Sportsman and the Man," whose energy and magnanimity were extolled in that essay. "The Wilderness Hunter" argued in less immediate detail that adventure was not dead in modern boys, while "The Open-Air Education" shows what, acted upon and made into a habit of mind and life, that spirit might do in redeeming America.

Wister had little hope in political solutions but, at this point, a good deal in individual *vertu*. In the mid-nineties he had been comforted by meeting "good men in the humbler walks of life" (*Owen Wister Out West*, 205), especially cowboys, "the manly, simple, humorous American type which I hold to be the best and bravest we possess and our hope in the future. They work hard, they play hard, and they don't go on strike" (246). They were, in fact, preindustrial, even pastoral. But the story he wrote about Dean Duke, the foreman of this particular outfit ("The Jimmyjohn Boss"; retitled "The Boy and the Buckaroos") was about the way in which cowboys can be controlled by superior intelligence and self-discipline, and in *The Virginian* he went even further in developing the portrait of a natural leader who raises himself to the position of coal magnate and one-man lateral trust—not exactly a Tweed or a Jay Gould, but hardly "a slim young giant, more beautiful than pictures."

By the time he finished *The Virginian* in 1902, Wister was an established family man and author, ready to put away the West and other memories of his protracted youth for the Jamesian novel *Lady Baltimore* (set in and extolling the virtues of the Old South) and for biographies of Grant and Washington. But in 1910, incapacitated for work and family life by a mysterious illness, he took refuge in a Wyoming cabin and soon got to the point where he could fish five hours a day, put himself on a schedule to write short personal letters, including descriptions of a scene "a good deal like Lohengrin," and lament to his wife that he had no "buoyancy . . . except what I manufacture for the sake of appearances; but certain hours here, chiefly when I am fishing along the river and surrounded by the lovely scenery, I do very much enjoy" (*That I May Tell*, 192). No wonder that he and Ernest Hemingway took to each other in the late twenties: Wister sounds like a somewhat more subtly traumatized Nick Adams on Big Two-Hearted River.

Out of this experience came the final stories for *Members of the Family*. The stories were not as nostalgic as the preface, but even Scipio Le Moyne is aware that he is not as young and carefree as he was, and Wister's experience with two of the men who helped him create the Virginian did not seem to indicate that their type would revitalize the East. George West, a guide on his first hunting expeditions, was so far from becoming a magnate "with a strong grip on many various enterprises" that his schemes for making money repeatedly failed, and Wister, having sent him cast-off clothes, money, and advice, finally refused any further help. West did marry an educated Bostonian and acquired some apartment houses in Seattle, but he was wiped out in the depression and became a janitor, though apparently a very dignified one. Corporal Charles D. Skirdin became a policeman in Philadelphia and was charged with murder after a warning shot fired during a gang disturbance ricocheted and killed a young man. As a character witness, Wister testified that "that man embodies all the characteristics of . . . 'The Virginian'" (Payne, 264), and Skirdin was acquitted, a pale forerunner of Dirty Harry.

By this time, Wister had entered what Darwin Payne calls

Wister's curmudgeon period, during which he wrote increasingly strident anti-German propaganda during and after the First World War and arguments for restricting immigration, took part in demonstrations against Franklin Delano Roosevelt, and found imaginative solace in European visits, long-standing club memberships, and memories. Most of us, as we get older, get less interesting. Wister got less interesting than most because, having helped to create the atmosphere of one period, he came merely to reflect that of another. But when he was almost seventy, he wrote to a friend that he had read *The Sun Also Rises* and "Fifty Grand" and added, "Were I thirty, that is the way I should wish to write" (Payne, 320). He backed his judgment, offering Hemingway financial support while he was struggling with *A Farewell to Arms,* and in fact he could write as well as he ever did: "Right Honorable the Strawberries" was included in *The Best Short Stories of 1927,* and some of the other tales in *When West Was West,* one of them including the first overtly psychedelic scene in American literature, are among his finest. Just before his death, a week after his seventy-eighth birthday, in 1938, he was at work on a book about wine.

Revisionists and those in search of lost American literature will find little in Wister to interest them. He did write a good deal that was not about the West, but even specialists like Darwin Payne find little to say about his poetry, biographical and political writing, or commentary on music. *The Virginian,* as popular opinion would have it, is his most highly finished and most compelling book. His other fiction, especially *Lin McLean* and a half-dozen short stories, contains striking scenes and descriptions, but Wister had what seems to be an incurable bent for melodrama, and his plots are at best serviceable and at worst embarrassing.

Of course, we are necessarily looking at him through the perspective of later writers like Hemingway and Edward Abbey. The conventions of style and technique which he employed affected the way he saw—and the way we see him. But if he took his cultural and social heritage with him, he did go, and he tried hard and often successfully to see this new world in a new way. His first—and best—impulse was to record, as Hemingway put it, "the people and the places and how the weather was." (*By-Line: Ernest Hemingway* [New York: Scribner's, 1967], 184.) He thought he was merely recording, and he does sketch quite vividly a world that was vanishing even as he watched. Of course, he was interpreting as well, and as that world slipped away he tried to understand what had happened in it and to it. In his final pieces, he tells not only how it felt, but how it felt to have felt it. This, not some operatic plot, was the real story that Wister had to tell, and his nonfiction tells it best.

The White Goat and His Country

Wister was a member of the executive committee, Theodore Roosevelt was president from the founding in 1888 until 1894, and several of their Harvard cronies were members of the Boone and Crockett Club, which sponsored the publication of the book in which this article appeared. Roosevelt and George Bird Grinnell outlined in their preface some of the practices of which the club disapproved ("all unsportsmanlike proceedings and all needless slaughter") and the principles upon which their love of hunting was based:

> Hunting big game in the wilderness is, above all things, a sport for a vigorous and masterful people. The rifle-bearing hunter . . . must be sound of body and firm of mind, and must possess energy, resolution, manliness, self-reliance, and capacity for hardy self-help. In short, the big-game hunter must possess qualities without which no race can do its life-work well. . . .

The Boone and Crockett Club sponsored an exhibit at the Chicago World's Fair, and it was involved in various conservation projects. (For further information, see Edmund Morris, The Rise of Theodore Roosevelt *[New York: Coward, McCann and Geohegan, 1979], 383–84.)*

At the annual dinner in 1894, Roosevelt outlined his objections to what he regarded as the graphic depiction of the eye-gouging incident in "Balaam and Pedro," which was softened for inclusion in The Virginian. *(See Wister's* Roosevelt: The Story of a Friendship 1880–1919 *[New York: Macmillan, 1930], 34.)*

The article was based on Wister's hunting trip of October–

November 1892. The trip to the hunting grounds is treated in some detail in the diary reprinted in Owen Wister Out West, *but the hunt itself is scarcely mentioned in the printed selections. Judging from letters by Roosevelt, Wister apparently wrote the article between April 4 and April 22, 1893. Several months later, Wister was asked to allow the removal of the anecdote about the Marquis of Lorne falling off his horse so that copies might be sold in England. He was inclined to agree, but I cannot discover whether the change was made.*

More important than any single anecdote or character in this account is the fact that Wister was discovering not only a new subject but a style, in fact, a voice or a persona, in which he could deal with it. In this piece, there are at least three styles. First and least attractive is the rather condescending comic diction used to describe the "sudden" new towns, the wild contrast between label and fact, and the Jews who do not fit in and the inhabitants who do. In this voice, Wister is both the insider and the outsider, sophisticate but not tenderfoot, a sort of apotheosis of the all-round Harvard man. (The voice is still with us in the essays of Tom Wolfe.) This voice tells a like-minded audience that the country cannot be appreciated by its inhabitants, and it is too rough for the merely civilized. The second voice sounds rather like someone trying to sell resort property: the generalized diction ("pleasant trees," "fertile soil," "purple cloak of forest" rising to "a crown of white, clean, frozen peaks") is not so much romantic as decayed eighteenth-century pastoral.

Both types of diction reveal conventional tastes—for civilized, sophisticated visitors over the inhabitants; for mountains over deserts—and both condescend to their subjects. It is not surprising that Wister should use this inherited vocabulary. It is surprising that he brought it to this country and that, once there, he should find a new one. A few pages after the feeble ecstasies about purple forests and pure white mountains, Wister is describing, as simply and precisely as Hemingway does Nick's camp along Big Two-Hearted River, the descent to a good place. He could not sustain this style or vision. For Nick Adams, the trout are just "there," in their own world. For Wister, "the goats should be

*where they ought to be" for the convenience of an American
gentleman of his particular caste.*

*However, Wister had begun to see more than the comedy and
the grandeur, more than the scientific data which he presents
rather stiffly (a real-life precursor of Charles Smithson in John
Fowles's* The French Lieutenant's Woman*), more even than the
process of securing hunting trophies. Comfortably camped in the
snowstorm, he can rejoice with some surprise at his successful
plagiarism of a Sibley stove and at gaining through it the respect of
T——. In turn, he presents, without condescending to them,
T——'s views on literature. The cook is negligible, but T—— is an
early, unromanticized version of the Virginian.*

*For a more rambling, garrulous, and unfocused version of some
of the same events, as well as a description of a later trip and some
scientific data, see Wister's "The White Goat and His Ways," in*
Musk-Ox, Bison, Sheep and Goat, *edited by George Bird Grinnell
and Caspar Whitney (New York: Macmillan Company for the
American Sportsman's Library, 1904).*

Source: American Big Game Hunting *(New York: Forest and
Stream Publishing Company, 1893), 26–60. Material about goats
as a species and some general reflections have been omitted.*

I N   A   C O R N E R of what is occasionally termed "Our Empire of
the Northwest," there lies a country of mountains and valleys
where, until recently, citizens have been few. At the present time
certain mines, and uncertain hopes, have gathered an eccentric
population and evoked some sudden towns. The names which
several of these bear are tolerably sumptuous: Golden, Oro, and
Ruby, for instance; and in them dwell many colonels and judges,
and people who own one suit of clothes and half a name (colored
by adjuncts, such as Hurry Up Ed), and who sleep almost anywhere. These communities are brisk, sanguine, and nomadic, full
of good will and crime; and in each of them you will be likely to
find a weekly newspaper, and an editor who is busy writing things
about the neighboring editors. The flume slants down the hill

bearing water to the concentrator; buckets unexpectedly swing out from the steep pines into mid-air, sailing along their wire to the mill; little new staring shanties appear daily; somebody having trouble in a saloon upsets a lamp, and half the town goes to ashes, while the colonels and Hurry Up Eds carouse over the fireworks till morning. In a short while there are more little shanties than ever, and the burnt district is forgotten. All this is going on not far from the mountain goat, but it is a forlorn distance from the railroad; and except for the stage line which the recent mining towns have necessitated, my route to the goat country might have been too prolonged and uncertain to attempt.

I stepped down one evening from the stage, the last public conveyance I was to see, after a journey that certainly has one good side. It is completely odious: and the breed of sportsmen that takes into camp every luxury excepting, perhaps, cracked ice, will not be tempted to infest the region until civilization has smoothed its path. The path, to be sure, does not roughen until one has gone along it for twenty-eight hundred miles. You may leave New York in the afternoon, and arrive very early indeed on the fifth day at Spokane. Here the luxuries begin to lessen, and a mean once-a-day train trundles you away on a branch west of Spokane at six in the morning into a landscape that wastes into a galloping consumption. Before noon the last sick tree, the ultimate starved blade of wheat, has perished from sight, and you come to the end of all things, it would seem; a domain of wretchedness unspeakable. Not even a warm, brilliant sun can galvanize the corpse of the bare ungainly earth. The railroad goes no further,—it is not surprising,—and the stage arranges to leave before the train arrives. Thus you spend sunset and sunrise in the moribund terminal town, the inhabitants of which frankly confess that they are not staying from choice. They were floated here by a boom-wave, which left them stranded. Kindly they were, and anxious to provide the stranger with what comforts existed.

Geographically I was in the "Big Bend" country, a bulk of land looped in by the Columbia River, and highly advertised by railroads for the benefit of "those seeking homes." Fruit and grain no doubt grow somewhere in it. What I saw was a desert cracked in two by a chasm sixty-five miles long. It rained in the night, and at seven next morning, bound for Port Columbia, we wallowed northward out of town in the sweating canvas-covered stage through primeval mud. After some eighteen miles we drew out of the rain area, and from around the wheels there immediately arose and came among us a primeval dust, monstrous, shapeless, and blind. First your power of speech deserted you, then your eyesight went, and at length you became uncertain whether you were alive. Then hilarity at the sheer discomfort overtook me, and I was joined in it by a brother American: but two Jew drummers on the back seat could not understand, and seemed on the verge of tears. The landscape was entirely blotted out by the dust. Often you could not see the roadside,—if the road had any side. We may have been passing homes and fruit-trees, but I think not. I remember wondering if getting goat after all—. But they proved well worth it.

Toward evening we descended into the sullen valley of the Columbia, which rushes along, sunk below the level of the desert we had crossed. High sterile hills flank its course, and with the sweeping, unfriendly speed of the stream, its bleak shores seemed a chilly place for home-seekers. Yet I blessed the change. A sight of running water once more, even of this overbearing flood, and of hills however dreary, was exhilaration after the degraded, stingy monotony of the Big Bend. The alkali trails in Wyoming do not seem paradises till you bring your memory of them here. Nor am I alone in my estimate of this impossible hole. There is a sign-post sticking up in the middle of it, that originally told the traveler it was thirty-five miles to Central Ferry. But now the traveler has retorted; and three different hand-writings on this sign-post reveal to you that you have had predecessors in your thought, comrades who shared your sorrows:

> Forty-five miles to water.
> Seventy-five miles to wood.

And then the last word:

> Two and one-half miles to hell.

Perhaps they were home-seekers.

We halted a moment at the town of Bridgeport, identified by

one wooden store and an inchoate hotel. The rest may be seen upon blue-print maps, where you would suppose Bridgeport was a teeming metropolis. At Port Columbia, which we reached by a landslide sort of road that slanted the stage over and put the twin Jew drummers in mortal fear, we slept in one of the two buildings which indicate that town. It is another important center,—in blue print,—but invisible to the naked eye. In the morning, a rope ferry floated the new stage and us travelers across the river. The Okanagon flows south from lakes and waters above the British line, and joins the Columbia here. We entered its valley at once, crossed it soon by another rope ferry, and keeping northward, with the river to the east between us and the Colville Reservation, had one good meal at noon, and entering a smaller valley, reached Ruby that evening. Here the stage left me to continue its way to Conconally, six miles further on. With the friends who had come to meet me, I ascended out of Ruby the next day over the abrupt hill westward, and passing one night out in my blankets near a hospitable but limited cabin (its flowing-haired host fed us, played us the fiddle, and would have had us sleep inside), arrived bag and baggage the fourth day from the railroad at the forks of the Methow River—the next tributary of the Columbia below the Okanagon.

Here was a smiling country, winning the heart at sight. An ample beauty was over everything Nature had accomplished in this place; the pleasant trees and clear course of the stream, a fertile soil on the levels, the slopes of the foot-hills varied and gentle, unencumbered by woods, the purple cloak of forest above these on the mountains, and rising from the valley's head a crown of white, clean frozen peaks. These are known to some as the Isabella Range and Mount Gardner, though the maps do not name them. Moreover, I heard that now I was within twenty-five miles of goats; and definite ridges were pointed out as the promised land.

Many things were said to me, first and last. I remember a ragged old trapper, lately come over the mountains from the Skagit River. Goats, did I say? On top there the goats had tangled your feet walking in the trail. He had shot two in camp for staring at him.

Another accurate observer had seen three hundred on a hill just above Early Winter as he was passing by. The cabined dwellers on the Methow tied their horses to the fence and talked to me—so I had come from the East after goats, had I?—and in the store of the Man at the Forks I became something of a curiosity. Day by day I sat on the kegs of nails, or lay along the counter devoted to his dry-goods, and heard what passed. Citizens and denizens—for the Siwash with his squaws and horses was having his autumn hunt in the valley—knocked at the door to get their mail, or buy tobacco, or sell horns and fur, or stare for an hour and depart with a grunt; and the grave Man at the Forks stood behind one counter while I lay on the other, acquiring a miscellaneous knowledge. One old medical gentleman had slain all wild animals without weapons, and had been the personal friend of so many distinguished histor-ical characters that we computed he was nineteen about the time of Bunker Hill. They were hospitable with their information, and I followed my rule of believing everything that I hear. And they were also hospitable with whatever they possessed. The memory of those distant dwellers among the mountains, young and old, is a friendly one, like the others I carry, whether of Wind or Powder Rivers, or the Yellowstone, or wherever Western trails have led me.

Yet disappointment and failure were the first things. There was all the zeal you could wish. We had wedged painfully into a severe country—twelve miles in two days, and trail-cutting between—when sickness turned us back, goatless. By this time October was almost gone, and the last three days of it went in patching up our disintegrated outfit. We needed other men and other horses; and while these were being sought, nothing was more usual than to hear "if we'd only been along with So-and-So, he saw goats" here and there, and apparently everywhere. We had, it would seem, ingeniously selected the only place where there were none. But somehow the services of So-and-So could not be procured. He had gone to town; or was busy getting his winter's meat; or his married daughter had just come to visit him, or he had married somebody else's daughter. I cannot remember the number of obstacles always lying between ourselves and So-and-So.

At length we were once more in camp on a stream named the Twispt. In the morning—new stroke of misfortune—one of us was threatened with illness, and returned to the Forks. We three, the guide, the cook, and myself, went on, finally leaving the narrow valley, and climbing four hours up a mountain at the rate of about a mile an hour. The question was, had winter come in the park above, for which we were heading? On top, we skirted a bare ridge from which everything fell precipitously away, and curving round along a steep hollow of the hill, came to an edge and saw the snow lying plentifully among the pines through which we must go down into the bottom of the park. But on the other side, where the sun came, there was little or none, and it was a most beautiful place. At the head of it was a little frozen lake fringed with tamarack, and a stream flowed down from this through scattered birches and pines, with good pasture for the horses between. The park sank at its outlet into a tall impassable cañon through which the stream joined the Twispt, miles below. It was a little lap of land clear at the top of the mountains, the final peaks and ridges of which rose all around, walling it in completely. You must climb these to be able to see into it, and the only possible approach for pack-horses was the pine-tree slant, down which we came. Of course there was no trail.

We prospected before venturing, and T——, the guide, shook his head. It was only a question of days—possibly of hours—when snow must shut the place off from the world until spring. But T—— appreciated the three thousand miles I had come for goats; and if the worst came to the worst, said he, we could "make it in" to the Forks on foot, leading the horses, and leaving behind all baggage that weighed anything. So we went down. Our animals slipped a little, the snow balling their feet; but nothing happened, and we reached the bottom and chose a camp in a clump of tamarack and pine. The little stream, passing through shadows here, ran under a lid of frozen snow easily broken, and there was plenty of wood, and on the ground only such siftings of snow as could be swept clean for the tent. The saddles were piled handily under a tree, a good fireplace was dug, we had a comfortable supper; and nothing remained but that the goats should be where they ought to be—on the ridges above the park.

I have slept more soundly; doubt and hope kept my thoughts active. Yet even so, it was pleasant to wake in the quiet and hear the bell on our horse, Duster, occasionally tankle somewhere on the hill. My watch I had forgotten to place at T——'s disposal, so he was reduced to getting the time of day from the stars. He consulted the Great Bear, and seeing this constellation at an angle he judged to indicate five o'clock, he came back into the tent, and I heard him wake the cook, who crawled out of his blankets.

"Why, it's plumb night," the cook whined.

"Make the breakfast," said T——.

I opened my eyes, and shut them immediately in despair at the darkness that I saw. Presently I heard the fire and the pans, and knew that the inevitable had come. So I got my clothes on, and we looked at my watch. It was only 4:30 A.M. T—— and the Great Bear had made half an hour's miscalculation, and the face of the cook was so grievous that I secretly laughed myself entirely awake. "Plumb night" lasted some time longer. I had leisure to eat two plates of oatmeal and maple syrup, some potato-and-onion soup, bacon, and coffee, and digest these, before dawn showed.

T—— and I left camp at 6:40 A.M. The day was a dark one. On the high peaks behind camp great mounds of cloud moved and swung, and the sky was entirely overcast. We climbed one of the lower ridges, not a hard climb nor long, but very sliding, and often requiring hands and feet to work round a ledge. From the top we could see the open country lying comfortably below and out of reach of the howling wind that cut across the top of the mountain, straight from Puget Sound, bringing all that it could carry of the damp of the Pacific. The ridges and summits that surrounded our park continually came into sight and disappeared again among the dense vapors which bore down upon them.

We went cautiously along the narrow top of crumbling slate, where the pines were scarce and stunted, and had twisted themselves into corkscrews so they might grip the ground against the tearing force of storms. We came on a number of fresh goat-tracks in the snow or the soft shale. These are the reverse of those of the mountain sheep, the V which the hoofs make having its open end in the direction the animal is going. There seemed to be several, large and small; and the perverted animals invariably chose the sharpest slant they could find to walk on, often with a decent level just beside it that we were glad enough to have. If there were a precipice and a sound flat top, they took the precipice, and crossed its face on juts that did not look as if your hat would hang on them. In this I think they are worse than the mountain sheep, if that is possible. Certainly they do not seem to come down into the high pastures and feed on the grass levels as the sheep will.

T—— and I hoped we should find a bunch, but that was not to be, in spite of the indications. As we continued, I saw a singular-looking stone lying on a little ledge some way down the mountain ahead. I decided it must be a stone, and was going to speak of it, when the stone moved, and we crouched in the slanting gravel. T—— had been making up his mind it was a stone. The goat turned his head our way, but did not rise. He was two hundred yards across a split in the mountain, and the wind blowing hard. T—— wanted me to shoot, but I did not dare to run such a chance. I have done a deal of missing at two hundred yards, and much nearer, too. So I climbed, or crawled, out of sight, keeping any stone or little bush between me and the goat, till I got myself where a buttress of rock hid me, and then I ran along the ridge and down and up the scoop in it made by the split of the mountain, and so came cautiously to where I could peer over and see the goat lying turned away from me, with his head commanding the valley. He was on a tiny shelf of snow, beside him was one small pine, and below that the rock fell away steeply into the gorge. Ought I to have bellowed at him, and at least have got him on his legs? I know it would have been more honorable. He looked white, and huge, and strange; and somehow I had a sense of personality about him more vivid than any since I watched my first silver-tip lift a rotten log, and, sitting on his hind legs, make a breakfast on beetles, picking them off the log with one paw.

I fired, aiming behind the goat's head. He did not rise, but turned his head round. The white bead of my Lyman sight had not showed well against the white animal, and I thought I had missed him. Then I fired again, and he rolled very little—six inches—and lay quiet. He could not have been more than fifty yards away, and my first shot had cut through the back of his neck and buried itself in mortal places, and the second in his head merely made death instantaneous. Shooting him after he had become alarmed might have lost him over the edge; even if a first shot had been fatal, it could not have been fatal soon enough. Two struggles on that snow would have sent him sliding through space. As it was, we had a steep, unsafe scramble down through the snow to where he lay stretched out on the little shelf by the tree.

He was a fair-sized billy, and very heavy. The little lifting and shoving we had to do in skinning him was hard work. The horns were black, slender, slightly spreading, curved backward, pointed, and smooth. They measured six inches round the base, and the distance from one point to the other, measured down one horn, along the skull, and up the other, was twenty-one and a half inches. The hoofs were also black and broad and large, wholly unlike a tame goat's. The hair was extraordinarily thick, long, and of a weather-beaten white; the eye large and deep-brown.

I had my invariable attack of remorse on looking closely at the poor harmless old gentleman, and wondered what achievement, after all, could be discerned in this sort of surprise and murder. We did not think of securing any of his plentiful fat, but with head and hide alone climbed back up the ticklish slant, hung the trophies on a tree in a gap on the camp side of the ridge, and continued our hunt. It was not ten o'clock yet, and we had taken one hour to skin the goat. We now hunted the higher ridges behind camp until 1 P.M., finding tracks that made it seem as if a number of goats must be somewhere near by. But the fog came down and shut everything out of sight; moreover, the wind on top blew so that we could not have seen had it been clear.

We returned to camp, and found it greatly improved. The cook had carpentered an important annex to the tent. By slanting pine-logs against a ridge-pole and nailing them, he had built a room, proof against wind and rain, and in it a table. One end was against the opening of the tent, the other at the fire. The arrangement was excellent, and timely also. The storm revived during the night, and it rained fitfully. The roar of the wind coming down from the mountain into our park sounded like a Niagara, and its approach was tremendous. We had built up a barrier of pine-brush, and this, with a clump of trees, sheltered us well enough; but there were wild moments when the gust struck us, and the tent shuddered and strained, until that particular breeze passed on with a diminishing roar down the cañon.

The next morning the rain kept us from making an early start, and we did not leave camp until eight. Now and then a drizzle fell from the mist, and the banks of clouds were still driving across the higher peaks, but during the day the sun slowly got the better of them. . . . The character of these mountainsides is such that even with the greatest care in stepping we sent a shower rattling down from time to time. We had a viciously bad climb. We went down through tilted funnels of crag, avoiding jumping off places by crossing slides of brittle slate and shale, hailing a dead tree as an oasis. And then we lost count, and T—— came unexpectedly on the goat, which was up and away and was shot by T—— before I could get a sight of him. I had been behind some twenty yards, both of us supposing we had to go considerably further. T—— was highly disgusted. "To think of me managing such a botch as that," he said, "when you've come so far"; and he wanted me to tell the people that I had shot the goat myself. He really cared more than I did.

This goat was also a billy, and larger than the first. We sat skinning him where he had fallen at the edge of a grove of tamarack, and T—— conversed about the royal family of England. He remarked that he had always rather liked "that chap Lorne."

I explained to him that "that chap Lorne" had made himself ridiculous forever at the Queen's Jubilee. Then, as T—— did not know, I told him how the marquis had insisted on riding in the procession upon a horse, against which the Prince of Wales, aware of the tame extent of his horsemanship, had warned him. In the middle of the pageant, the Queen in her carriage, the crowned heads of Europe escorting her on horseback, and the whole world looking on—at this picturesque moment, Lorne fell off. I was not sure that T—— felt fully how inappropriate a time this was for a marquis to tumble from his steed.

"I believe the Queen sent somebody," I continued.

"Where?" said T——.

"To him. She probably called the nearest king and said: 'Frederick, Lorne's off. Go and see if he's hurt.'"

" 'And if he ain't hurt, *hurt him*,' " said T——, completing her Majesty's thought.

This second billy seemed to me twice the size of a domestic goat. . . . After all, the comparison is one into which we are misled by the name. This is an antelope; and though, through certain details of his costume, he is able to masquerade as a goat, it must be remembered that he is of a species wholly distinct.

We took the web tallow, and the tallow of one kidney. The web was three quarters of an inch thick.

Neither elk, nor any animal I have seen, except bear, has such quantities of fat, and I do not think even a bear has a thicker hide. On the rump it was as thick as the sole of my boot, and the masses of hair are impenetrable to anything but modern firearms. An arrow might easily stick harmless; and I am told that carnivorous animals who prey upon the deer in these mountains respectfully let the goat alone. Besides his defensive armor, he is an ugly customer in attack. He understands the use of his thin, smooth horns, and, driving them securely into the belly of his enemy, jumps back and leaves him a useless, ripped-open sack. Male and female have horns of much the same size; and in taking a bite out of one of either sex, as T—— said, a mountain lion would get only a mouthful of hair. . . .

I wished to help carry the heavy hide of the second billy; but T—— inflicted this upon himself, "every step to camp," he insisted, "for punishment at disappointing you." The descent this day had been bad enough, taking forty minutes for some four hundred yards. But now we were two hours getting up, a large part of the way on hands and knees. I carried the two rifles and the glass, going in front to stamp some sort of a trail in the sliding rocks, while T—— panted behind me, bearing the goat-hide on his back.

Our next hunt was from seven till four, up and down, in the presence of noble and lonely mountains. The straight peaks which marshal round the lake of Chelan were in our view near by, beyond the valley of the Twispt, and the whole Cascade range rose endlessly, and seemed to fill the world. Except in Switzerland, I have never seen such an unbroken area of mountains. And all this beauty going begging, while each year our American citizens of the East, more ignorant of their own country and less identified with its soil than any race upon earth, herd across the sea to the tables d'hôte they know by heart! But this is wandering a long way from goats, of which this day we saw none.

A gale set in after sunset. This particular afternoon had been so mellow, the sun had shone so clear from a stable sky, that I had begun to believe the recent threats of winter were only threats, and that we had some open time before us still. Next morning we waked in midwinter, the flakes flying thick and furious over a park that was no longer a pasture, but a blind drift of snow. We lived in camp, perfectly comfortable. Down at the Forks I had had made a rough imitation of a Sibley stove. All that its forger had to go on was my unprofessional and inexpert description, and a lame sketch in pencil; but he succeeded so well that the hollow iron cone and joints of pipe he fitted together turned out most efficient. The sight of the apparatus packed on a horse with the panniers was whimsical, and until he saw it work I know that T—— despised it. After that, it commanded his respect. All this stormy day it roared and blazed, and sent a lusty heat throughout the tent. T—— cleaned the two goat-heads, and talked Shakspere and Thackeray to me. He quoted Henry the Fourth, and regretted that Thackeray had not more developed the character of George Warrington. Warrington was the *man* in the book. When night came the storm was gone.

By eight the next morning we had sighted another large solitary billy. But he had seen us down in the park from his ridge. He had come to the edge, and was evidently watching the horses. If not quick-witted, the goat is certainly wary; and the next time we saw him he had taken himself away down the other side of the mountain, along a spine of rocks where approach was almost impossible. We watched his slow movements through the glass, and were both reminded of a bear. He felt safe, and was stepping deliberately along, often stopping, often walking up some small point and surveying the scenery. He moved in an easy, rolling fashion, and turned his head importantly. Then he lay down in the sun, but saw us on our way to him, and bounced off. We came to the place where he had jumped down sheer twenty feet at least. His hoof-tracks were on the edge, and in the gravel below the heavy scatter he made in landing; and then,—hasty tracks round a corner of rock, and no more goat that day.

I had become uneasy about the weather. It was all sunshine again, and though our first goat was irretrievably gone, we had the afternoon before us. Nevertheless, when I suggested we should spend it in taking the shoes off the horses, so they might be able to walk homeward without falling in the snow, T—— thought it our best plan. We wanted to find a bunch of goats now, nannies and kids, as well as billies. It had been plain that these ridges here contained very few, and those all hermits; males who from age, or temperament, or disappointment in love, had retired from society, and were spending the remainder of their days in a quiet isolation and whatever is the goat equivalent for reading Horace. It was well enough to have begun with these philosophers, but I wanted new specimens.

We were not too soon. A new storm had set in by next morning, and the unshod horses made their journey down the mountain, a most odious descent for man and beast, in the sliding snow. But down on the Twispt it was yet only autumn, with no snow at all. This was a Monday, the 7th of November, and we made haste to the Forks, where I stopped a night to read a large, accumulated mail, and going on at once, overtook my outfit, which had preceded me on the day before.

Our new camp—and our last one—was up the Methow, twenty-three miles above the Forks, in a straight line. Here the valley split at right angles against a tall face of mountain, and each way the stream was reduced to a brook one could cross afoot. The new valley became steep and narrow almost at once, and so continued to the divide between Columbia water and tributaries of the Skagit. We lived comfortably in an old cabin built by prospectors. The rain filtered through the growing weeds and sand on the roof and dropped on my head in bed; but not much, and I was able to steer it off by a rubber blanket. And of course there was no glass in the windows; but to keep out wind and wet we hung gunny sacks across those small holes, and the big stone fireplace was magnificent.

By ten next morning T—— and I saw "three hundred" goats on the mountain opposite where we had climbed. Just here I will risk a generalization. When a trapper tells you he has seen so many hundred head of game, he has not counted them, but he believes what he says. The goats T—— and I now looked at were a mile away in an air-line, and they seemed numberless. The picture which the white, slightly moving dots made, like mites on a cheese, inclined one to a large estimate of them, since they covered the whole side of a hill. The more we looked the more we found; besides the main army there were groups, caucuses, families sitting apart over some discourse too intimate for the general public; and beyond these single animals could be discerned, moving, gazing, browsing, lying down.

"Megod and Begod," said T—— (he occasionally imitated a brogue for no hereditary reason), "there's a hundred thousand goats!"

"Let's count 'em," I suggested, and we took the glasses. There were thirty-five.

We found we had climbed the wrong hill, and the day was too short to repair this error. Our next excursion, however, was successful. The hill where the goats were was not two miles above camp,—you could have seen the animals from camp but for the curve in the cañon,—yet we were four hours and a half climbing the ridge, in order to put ourselves above them. It was a hard climb, entirely through snow after the first. On top the snow came at times considerably above the knees. But the judicious T—— (I have never hunted with a more careful and thorough man) was right in the route he had chosen, and after we had descended again to the edge of the snow, we looked over a rock, and saw, thirty yards below us, the nanny and kid for which we had been aiming. I should have said earlier that the gathering of yesterday had dispersed during the night, and now little bunches of three and four goats could be seen up and down the cañon. We were on the exact ground they had occupied, and their many tracks were plain. My first shot missed—thirty yards!—and as nanny and kid went bounding by on the hill below, I knocked her over with a more careful bullet, and T—— shot the kid. The little thing was not dead when we came up, and at the sight of us it gave a poor little thin bleat that turns me remorseful whenever I think of it. We had all the justification that any code exacts. We had no fresh meat, and among goats the kid alone is eatable; and I justly desired specimens of the entire family.

We carried the whole kid to camp, and later its flesh was excellent. The horns of the nanny, as has been said before, are but slightly different from those of the male. They are, perhaps, more slender, as is also the total makeup of the animal. In camp I said to T—— that I desired only one more of those thirty-five goats, a billy; and that if I secured him the next day, that should be the last. Fortune was for us. We surprised a bunch of several. They had seen me also, and I was obliged to be quick. This resulted in some shots missing, and in two, perhaps three, animals going over ledges with bullets in them, leaving safe behind the billy I wanted. His conduct is an interesting example of the goat's capacity to escape you and die uselessly, out of your reach.

I had seen him reel at my first shot, but he hurried around a corner, and my attention was given to others. As I went down, I heard a shot, and came round the corner on T——, who stood some hundred yards further along the ledge beside a goat. T—— had come on him lying down. He had jumped up and run apparently unhurt, and T—— had shot him just as he reached the end of the ledge. Beyond was a fall into inaccessible depths. Besides T——'s shot we found two of mine—one clean through from the shoulder—the goat had faced me when I fired first—to the ham, where the lead was flat against the bone. This goat was the handsomest we had, smaller than the other males, but with horns of a better shape, and with hair and beard very rich and white. Curiously enough, his lower jaw between the two front teeth had been broken a long time ago, probably from some fall. Yet this accident did not seem to have interfered with his feeding, for he was in excellent plump condition.

This completely satisfied me, and I willingly decided to molest no more goats. I set neither value nor respect on numerical slaughter. One cannot expect Englishmen to care whether American big game is exterminated or not; that Americans should not care is a disgrace. The pervading spirit of the far West as to game, as to timber, as to everything that a true American should feel it his right to use and his duty to preserve for those coming after, is— "What do I care, so long as it lasts my time?" . . .

The Evolution of the Cow-Puncher

As Ben Merchant Vorpahl has shown (My Dear Wister), *this essay was written at the insistence and with the aid of Frederic Remington, who illustrated it for* Harper's Monthly.

The essay is more valuable as an indication of Wister's characteristic prejudices—which reflected and still reflect a strong if inchoate ethos—than as an indication of any historical reality. And though some of the material may have come from field research, nothing in the essay compares with the direct observation in "The White Goat" or even "Educating the Polo Pony." In other words, observation has been filtered through or replaced by ideology.

It is not a very coherent ideology. The view that the western population was selected and adapted to the needs of the environment, implicit in much of Wister's writing, looks like a variety of social Darwinism, but, looked at closely, the essay in fact denies evolutionary process because "the slumbering untamed Saxon" persists through various successive conditions. And only the Saxon is able to survive on the plains because of superior wildness—or, in view of the awkward fact that the cowboy derived from the vaquero, perhaps superior moral qualities.

The emotional confusion is even more pervasive than the intellectual confusion. Wister owes an obvious debt to the Walter Scott version of romance, but though he professes to regret the absence of women suitable to a romance, he clearly regards women as irrelevant to the Saxon knight/cowpuncher. And though he speaks of the Saxon as preparing the way for civilization, he is more interested in robust vice than in pale virtue and, in fact, regards civilization, at least in the United States, as becoming inevitably base. The West, he strongly implies, was better left a playground for the carefree Saxon nomad rather than becoming a home for the grubbing, ignorant Populist or the site of crowded, boring, threatening cities which had no place either for the cowboy or the English lord—or the American gentleman. He was against pollution, but he was more interested in social than in environmental pollution.

In fact, Wister came to feel that the West was not so much a place in which moral qualities were created as one in which they were tested. But these uncertainties and even outbreaks of sheer nonsense do nothing to displace the essay from its central position in the mythology of the West that persists even now in country and western songs like "The Last Cowboy Song," "Pancho and Lefty," and "Mamas, Don't Let Your Babies Grow Up to Be Cowboys." Like the authors and singers of these songs, though in more gentlemanly and elitist language, Wister was really trying to find, preserve, and celebrate his own wilder impulses.

The outlaw mentioned at the end of the essay is Henry Smith, whose career and language Wister recorded in his diary for 1891 (Owen Wister Out West, 106, 117–18).

Source: Harper's Monthly 91 (September 1895): 602–17. Reprinted in the collected edition of Red Men and White (New York: Macmillan, 1928). The latter text is reproduced here.

TWO MEN sat opposite me once, despising each other so heartily that I am unlikely to forget them. They had never met before—if they can be said to have met this time—and they were both unknown to me. It happened in a train by which we journeyed together from Leamington to London. The cause of their mutual disesteem was appearance; neither liked the other's outward man, and told him so silently for three hours; that is all they ever knew of each other. This object-lesson afterward gained greatly by my learning the name and estate of one of these gentlemen. He was a peer. He had good rugs, a good umbrella, several newspapers—but read only the pink one,—and a leather and silver thing which I took to be a travelling-bag beside him. He opened it between Banbury and Oxford, and I saw, not handkerchiefs and ivory, but cut-glass bottles with stoppers. I noticed further the strong sumptuous monogram engraved here and there. The peer leisurely took brandy, and was not aware of our presence. But the point of him is that he garnished those miles of railroad with incomparably greater comfort than we did who had no rugs, no cut glass, no sandwich-box, no monogram. He had understood life's upholstery and trappings for several hundred years, getting the best to be had in each generation of his noble descent.

The enemy that he had made, as a dog makes an enemy of a cat by the mere preliminary of being a dog, sat in the other corner. He wore a shiny silk hat, smooth new lean black trousers, with high boots stiff and swelling to stove-pipe symmetry beneath, and a tie devoid of interest. I did not ascertain if the pistol was in his hip pocket, but at stated intervals he spit out of his window. By his hawk nose and eye and the lank strength of his chin he was a male who could take care of himself, and had done so. One could be sure he had wrested success from this world somehow, somewhere; and here he was; in a first-class carriage on a first-class train, come for a first-class time, with a mind as complacently shut against being taught by foreign travel as any American patriot of to-day can attain or recommend, or any Englishman can reveal in his ten-day book about our continent and people. Charles Dickens and Mark Twain have immortalized their own blindness almost equally; and the sad truth is that enlightenment is mostly a stay-at-home creature, who crosses neither ocean nor frontier. This stranger was of course going to have a bad time, and feel relieved to get home and tell of the absence of baggage-checks and of the effete despot who had not set up the drinks. Once he addressed the despot, who was serenely smoking.

"I'll trouble you for a light," said he; and in his drawl I heard plainly his poor opinion of feudalism.

His lordship returned the drawl—not audibly, but with his eye, which he ran slowly up and down the stranger. His was the

Piccadilly drawl; the other made use of the trans-Missouri variety; and both these are at bottom one and the same—the Anglo-Saxon's note of eternal contempt for whatever lies outside the beat of his personal experience. So I took an observation of these two Anglo-Saxons drawling at each other across the prejudice of a hundred years, and I thought it might come to a row. For the American was, on the quiet face of him, a "bad man," and so, to any save the provincial eye, was the nobleman. Fine feathers had deceived trans-Missouri, whose list of "bad men" was limited to specimens of the cut of his own jib, who know nothing of cut-glass bottles. But John gave Jonathan the light he asked, and for the remainder of our journey ceased to know that such a person existed.

Though we three never met again, my object-lesson did not end when we parted at Paddington. Before many seasons were sped the fortunes of the nobleman took a turn for the scandalous. He left cut glass behind him and went to Texas. I wish I could veraciously tell that he saw the stranger there—the traveller between whose bird-of-freedom nostrils and the wind his luxurious nobility had passed so offensively. But I do know that his second and more general skirmish with democracy left both sides amicable. In fact, the nobleman won the Western heart forthwith. Took it by surprise; democracy had read in the papers so often about the despot and his effeteness. This despot vaulted into the saddle and stuck to the remarkably ingenious ponies that had been chosen with care to disconcert him. When they showed him pistols, he was found to be already acquainted with that weapon. He quickly learned how to rope a steer. The card habit ran in his noble blood as it did in the cow-boy's. He could sleep on the ground and rough it with the best of them, and with the best of them he could drink and help make a town clamorous. Deep in him lay virtues and vices coarse and elemental as theirs. Doubtless the windows of St. James Street sometimes opened in his memory, and he looked into them and desired to speak with those whom he saw inside. And the whisky was not like the old stuff in the cut-glass bottles; but he never said so; and in time he died, widely esteemed. Texas found no count against him save his pronunciation of such words as bath and fancy—a misfortune laid to the accident of his birth; and you will hear to-day in that flannel-shirted democracy only good concerning this aristocrat born and bred.

Now, besides several morals which no pious person will find difficult to draw from the decline and fall of this aristocrat, there is something more germane to my democratic contemplation: after all, when driven to flock with our Wild West, he was a bird of that wild feather. That is the object-lesson; that is the gist of the matter. Directly the English nobleman smelt Texas, the slumbering untamed Saxon awoke in him, and mindful of the tournament, mindful of the hunting-field, galloped howling after wild cattle, a born horseman, a perfect athlete, and spite of the peerage and gules and argent, fundamentally kin with the drifting vagabonds who swore and galloped by his side. The man's outcome typifies the way of his race from the beginning. Hundreds like him have gone to Australia, Canada, India, and have done likewise, and in our own continent you may see the thing plainer than anywhere else. No rood of modern ground is more debased and mongrel with its hordes of encroaching alien vermin, that turn our cities to Babels and our citizenship to a hybrid farce, who degrade our commonwealth from a nation into something half pawn-shop, half broker's office. But to survive in the clean cattle country requires spirit of adventure, courage, and self-sufficiency; you will not find many Poles or Huns or Russian Jews in that district; but the Anglo-Saxon is still forever homesick for out-of-doors.

Throughout his career it has been his love to push further into the wilderness, and his fate thereby to serve larger causes than his own. In following his native bent he furthers unwittingly a design outside himself; he cuts the way for the common law, and self-government; and new creeds, polities and nations arise in his wake; in his own immense commonwealth this planless rover is obliterated. Roving took him (the Viking portion of him) from his Norse crags across to Albion. From that hearth of Albion the footprints of his sons lead to the corners of the earth; beside that hearth how inveterate remains his flavor! At Hastings he tasted defeat, but was not vanquished; to the Invincible Armada he proved a grievous surprise; one way or another he came through

Waterloo—possibly because he is inveterately dull at perceiving himself beaten; when not otherwise busy at Balaklava or by the Alma, he is getting up horse-races, ready for sport or killing—and all with that silver and cut-glass finish which so offends our noisy, empty-minded democracy. Greatest triumph and glory of all, because spiritual, his shoulders bore the Reformation when its own originators had tottered. Away from his hearth, the cut-glass stage will not generally have been attained by him; and in Maine or Kentucky you can recognize at sight the chip of the old rough block. But if you meet him upon his island, in the shape of a peer, and find him particular to dress for dinner seven days of the week, do not on that account imagine that his white tie has throttled the man in him. That is a noisy Fourth-of-July misconception. It's no symptom of patriotism to be unable to see a man through cut glass, and if it comes to an appraisement of the stranger and the peer, I should say, put each in the other's place, and let us see if the stranger could play the peer as completely as the peer played the cowboy. Sir Francis Drake was such a one; and Raleigh, the fine essence of Anglo-Saxon, with his fashionable gallant cloak, his adventure upon new seas, and his immediate appreciation of tobacco. The rover may return with looted treasure, or with incidentally stolen corners of territory to clap in his strong-box (this Angle is no angel), but it is not the dollars that played first fiddle with him, else our Hebrew friends would pioneer the whole of us. Adventure, to be out-of-doors, to find some new place far away from the postman, to enjoy independence of spirit or mind or body (according to his high or low standards)—this is the cardinal surviving fittest instinct that makes the Saxon through the centuries conqueror, invader, navigator, buccaneer, explorer, colonist, tiger-shooter; lifts him a pilgrim among the immortals at Plymouth Rock, dangles him a pirate from the gallows on the docks of Bristol. At all times when historic conditions or private stress have driven or tempted him from his hearth, there he is, making love to Pocahontas, or praying on Plymouth Rock, or shooting across the Missouri, or sailing up the Columbia, a Hawkins, a Boone, a Grey, or a nameless vagrant, the same Saxon, ploughing the seas and carving the forests, but in every shape a man, from preacher to thief, and in each shape changelessly untamed. And as he has ruled the waves with his ship from that Viking time until yesterday at Samoa, when approaching death could extract no sound from him save American cheers and music, so upon land has the horse been his foster-brother, his ally, his playfellow, from the tournament at Camelot to the round-up at Abilene, where he learned quickly what the Mexican vaquero had to teach him. The blood and the sweat of his jousting, and all the dirt and stains, have faded in the long sunlight of tradition, and in the chronicles of romance we hear none of his curses or obscenity; the clash of his armor rings mellow and heroic down the ages into our modern ears. But his direct lineal offspring among our Western mountains has had no poet to connect him with the eternal, no distance to lend him enchantment; though he has fought single-handed with savages, and through skill and daring prevailed, though he has made his nightly bed in a thousand miles of snow and loneliness, he has not, and never will have, the "consecration of memory." No doubt Sir Launcelot bore himself with a grace and breeding of which our unpolished fellow of the cattle trail has only the latent possibility; but in personal daring and in skill as to the horse, the knight and the cowboy are nothing but the same Saxon of different environments, the polished man in London and the man unpolished in Texas; and no hoof in Sir Thomas Malory shakes the crumbling plains with quadruped sound more valiant than the galloping that has echoed from the Rio Grande to the Big Horn Mountains. But we have no Sir Thomas Malory!

From the tournament to the round-up! Deprive the Saxon of his horse, and put him to forest-clearing or in a countinghouse for a couple of generations, and you may pass him by without ever seeing that his legs are designed for the gripping of saddles. Our first hundred years afforded his horsemanship but little opportunity. Though his out-of-door spirit, most at home when at large, sported free in the elbow-room granted by the surrender of Cornwallis, it was on foot and with an axe he chiefly enjoyed himself. He moved his log cabin slowly inward from the Atlantic, slowly over the wooded knolls of Cumberland and Allegheny, down and across the valley beyond, until the infrequent news of him ceased, and his kinsfolk who had staid by the sea, and were merchanting themselves upwards to the level of family portraits and the cut-glass finish, forgot that the prodigal in the backwoods belonged to them, and was part of their United States, bone of their bone. And thus did our wide country become as a man whose East hand knoweth not what his West hand doeth.

Mr. Herndon, in telling of Lincoln's early days in Illinois, gives us a complete picture of the roving Saxon upon our continent in 1830. "The boys . . . were a terror to the entire region—seemingly a necessary product of frontier civilization. They were friendly and good-natured. . . . They would do almost anything for sport or fun, love or necessity. Though rude and rough, though life's forces ran over the edge of their bowl, foaming and sparkling in pure deviltry for deviltry's sake, . . . yet place before them a poor man who needed their aid, . . . a defenseless woman, . . . they melted into sympathy and charity at once. They gave all they had, and willingly toiled or played cards for more. . . . A stranger's introduction was likely to be the most unpleasant part of his acquaintance. . . . They were in the habit of 'cleaning out' New Salem." Friendly and good-natured, and in the habit of cleaning out New Salem! Quite so. There you have him. Here is the American variety of the Saxon set down for you as accurately as if Audubon himself had done it. A Sheriff of Nottingham should go on the opposite page. Nothing but the horse is left out of the description, and that is because the Saxon and his horse seldom met during the rail-splitting era of our growth. But the man of 1830 would give away all that he had and play cards for more. Decidedly nothing was missing except the horse—and the horse was waiting in another part of our large map until the man should arrive and jump on his back again.

A few words about this horse—the horse of the plains. Whether or not his forefathers looked on when Montezuma fell, they certainly hailed from Spain. And whether it was missionaries or thieves who carried them northward from Mexico, until the Sioux heard of the new animal, certain it also is that this pony ran wild for a century or two, either alone or with various red-skinned owners; and as he gathered the sundry experiences of war and peace, of being stolen, and of being abandoned in the snow at inconvenient distances from home, of being ridden by two women and a baby at once, and of being eaten by a bear, his wide range of misadventure brought him a wit sharper than the street Arab's and an attitude towards life more spontaneously cynical and blasé than you can readily match in the united capitals of Europe. I have frequently caught him watching me with an eye of such sardonic depreciation that I felt it quite vain to attempt any hiding from him of my incompetence; and as for surprising him, a locomotive cannot do it, for I have tried this. He relishes putting a man in absurd positions, and will wait many days in patience to compass this uncharitable thing; and when he cannot bring a man to derision, he contents himself with a steer or a buffalo, helping the man to rope and throw these animals with an ingenuity surpassing any circus, to my thinking. A number of delighted passengers on the Kansas Pacific Railway passed by a Mexican vaquero, who had been sent out from Kansas City to rope a buffalo as an advertisement for the stock-yards. The train stopped to take a look at the solitary horseman fast to a buffalo in the midst of the plains. José, who had his bull safely roped, shouted to ask if they had water on the train. "We'll bring you some," said they. "Oh, I come get," said he; and jumping off, he left his accomplished pony in sole charge of the buffalo. Whenever the huge beast struggled for freedom, the clever pony stiffened his legs and leaned back as in a tug of war, by jumps and dodges so anticipating each move of the enemy, that escape was entirely hopeless. The boy got his drink, and his employer sent out a car for the buffalo, which was taken in triumph into Kansas City behind the passenger train. The Mexican narrated the exploit to his employer thus: "Oh Shirley, when the train start they all give three greata big cheers for me, and then give three mucha bigger cheers for the little gray hoss!"

Ah, progress is truly a wonder! and admirable beyond all doubt it is to behold the rapid new square miles of brick, and the stream rich with contributions of an increased population, and tall factories that have stopped dividends just for the present, and long empty railroads in the hands of the receiver; but I prefer that unenlightened day when we had moderate money and cheered for the little gray hoss.

Such was the animal that awaited the coming of the rail-splitter. The meeting was a long way off in 1830. Not the Mexican war, not the gold on the Pacific in '49 (though this, except for the horse, revealed the whole Saxon at his best and worst, and for a brief and beautiful moment waked once more the true voice of the American muse), not any national event until the War of the Rebellion was over and we had a railroad from coast to coast, brought the man and his horse together. It was in the late sixties that this happened in Texas. The adventurous sons of Kentucky and Tennessee, forever following the native bent to roam, and having no longer a war to give them the life they preferred, came into a new country full of grass and cattle. Here they found Mexicans by the hundred, all on horses and at large over the flat of the world. This sight must have stirred memories in the rail-splitter's blood, for he joined the sport upon the instant. I do not think he rode with bolder skill than the Mexicans, but he brought other and grittier qualities to bear upon that wild life, and also the Saxon contempt for the foreigner. Soon he had taken what was good from this small, deceitful alien, including his name, Vaquero, which he translated into Cow-boy. He took his saddle, his bridle, his spurs, his rope, his methods of branding and herding—indeed, most of his customs and accoutrements—and with them he went rioting over the hills. His playground was two thousand miles long and a thousand wide. The hoofs of his horse were tough as iron, and the pony waged the joyous battle of self-preservation as stoutly as did his rider. When the man lay rolled in his blankets sleeping, warm and unconcerned beneath a driving storm of snow, the beast pawed through to the sage-brush and subsisted; so that it came to be said of such an animal, "A meal a day is enough for a man who gets to ride that horse."

The cow-puncher's play-ground in those first glorious days of his prosperity included battle and murder and sudden death as every-day matters. From 1865 to 1878 in Texas he fought his way with knife and gun, and any hour of the twenty-four might see him flattened behind the rocks among the whizz of bullets and the flight of arrows, or dragged bloody and folded together from some adobe hovel. Seventy-five dollars a month and absolute health and strength were his wages; and when the news of all this excellence drifted from Texas eastward, they came in shoals— Saxon boys of picked courage (none but plucky ones could survive) from South and North, from town and country. Every sort and degree of home tradition came with them from their far birthplaces. Some had knelt in the family prayers at one time, others could remember no parent or teacher except the street; some spoke with the gentle accent of Virginia, others in the dialect of baked beans and codfish; here and there was the baccalaureate, already beginning to forget his Greek alphabet, but still able to repeat the two notable words with which Xenophon always marches upon the next stage of his journey. Hither to the cattle country they flocked from forty kinds of home, each bringing a deadly weapon.

What motlier tribe, what heap of cards shuffled from more various unmatched packs, could be found? Yet this tribe did not remain motley, but soon grew into a unit. To begin with, the old spirit burned alike in all, the unextinguished fire of adventure and independence. And then, the same stress of shifting for self, the same vigorous and peculiar habits of life, were forced upon each one: watching for Indians, guarding huge herds at night, chasing cattle, wild as deer, over rocks and counties, sleeping in the dust and waking in the snow, cooking in the open, swimming the swollen rivers. Thus late in the nineteenth century, was the race once again subjected to battles and darkness, to nature in the raw, to the fierceness and generosity of the desert. Destiny tried her latest experiment upon the Saxon and plucking him from the library, the haystack, and the gutter, set him upon his horse; then it was that, face to face with the eternal simplicity of death, his modern guise fell away and showed once again the mediaeval man. It was no new type, no product of the frontier, but just the original kernel of the nut with the shell broken.

This bond of adventure unified the divers young men, who came from various points of the compass, speaking university and gutter English simultaneously; and as the knights of Camelot

prized their armor and were particular about their swords, so
these dusty successors had an extreme pride of equipment, and
put aside their jeans and New York suits for the tribal dress.
Though each particle of gearing for man and horse was evoked
from daily necessity, gold and silver instantly stepped in to play
their customary ornamental part, as with all primitive races. The
cow-puncher's legs must be fended from the thorny miles of the
Rio Grande, the thousand mongrel shrubs that lace their bristles
together stiff over the face of the country—the mesquite, the shin-
oak, the cat's-claw; the Spanish-dagger, spread wide, from six
inches to ten feet high; every vegetable vicious with its equipment
of teeth and nails; a continent of peevish thicket called chaparral,
as we indiscriminately call a dog with too many sorts of grand-
fathers a cur. Into this saw-mill dives the wild steer through paths
and passages known to himself, and after him the pursuing man;
his flesh would be shredded to ribbons if the blades and points
could get hold of him; but he cases his legs against the hostile
chaparral from thigh to ankle in chaps—leathern breeches, next
door to armor; his daily bread is scarcely more needful to him.
Soon his barbaric pleasure in finery sews tough leather fringe
along their sides, and the leather flap of the pocket becomes
stamped with a heavy rose. Sagging in a slant upon his hips leans
his leather belt of cartridges buckled with jaunty arrogance, and
though he uses his pistol with murderous skill, it is pretty, with
ivory or mother-of-pearl for a handle. His arm must be loose to
swing his looped rope free and drop its noose over the neck of the
animal that bounds in front of his rushing pony. Therefore he
rides in a loose flannel shirt that will not cramp him as he whirls
the coils; but the handkerchief knotted at his throat, though it is
there to prevent sunburn, to shield his face, and to use in precipi-
tate moments, will in time of prosperity be chosen for its color and
soft texture—a scarf to draw the eye of woman. His heavy splendid saddle is in its shape and luxury of straps and leather thongs,
the completest instrument for night and day travel, and the
freighting along with you of board and lodging, that any nomad
has so far devised. With its trappings and stamped leather, its horn
and high cantle, we are well acquainted. It must stand the strain of

eight hundred pounds of live beef suddenly tearing at it for freedom; it must be the anchor that shall not drag during the furious rages of such a typhoon. For the cattle of the wilderness have often run wild for three, four, and five years, through rocks and forests, never seeing the face of man from the day when as little calves they were branded. And some were never branded at all. They have grown up in company with the deer, and like the deer they fly at the approach of the horseman. Then, if he has ridden out to gather these waifs from their remote, untenanted pastures, and bring them in to be counted and driven to sale, he must abandon himself to the headlong pursuit. The open easy plain with its harmless footing lies behind, the steep valley narrows up to an entering wedge among the rocks, and into these untoward regions rush the beeves. The shale and detritus of shelving landslide, the slippery knobs in the beds of brooks, the uncertain edges of the jumping-off place, all lie in the road of the day's necessity, and where the steer goes, goes the cow-puncher too—balancing, swaying, doubling, whirling upon his shrewd pony. The noose uncoiling flies swinging through the air and closes round the throat—or perhaps only the hind leg—of the quarry. In the shock of stopping short or of leaning to circle, the rider's stirrups must be long, and his seat a forked pliant poise on the horse's back; no grip of the knee will answer in these contortions; his leg must have its straight length, a lever of muscle and sinew to yield or close viselike on the pony's ribs; and when the steer feels that he is taken and the rope tightens from the saddle horn, then must the gearing be solid, else, like a fisherman floundering with snapped rod and tangled line, the cow-puncher will have misfortunes to repair and nothing to repair them with. Such a thing as this has happened in New Mexico: The steer, pursued and frantic at feeling the throttle of the flung rope, ran blindly over a cliff, one end of the line fast to him, the other to the rider's saddle horn, and no time to think once, much less twice, about anything in this or the next world. The pony braced his legs at the edge, but his gait swept him onward, as with the fast skater whose skate has stuck upon a frozen chip. The horse fell over the mountain, and with him his rider; but the sixty-foot rope was new, and it hooked over a stump. Steer and horse swung like scales gently above the man, who lay at the bottom, hurt nearly to death, but not enough to dull his appreciation of the unusual arrangement. It is well, then, to wear leathern armor and sit in a stout saddle if you would thrive among the thorns and rocks; and without any such casualty as falling over a mountain, the day's common events call for uncommon strength of gear. Not otherwise can the steer be roped and landed safely, and not otherwise is the man to hoist resisting beeves up a hill, somewhat as safes are conducted to the sixth story; nor could the rider plunge galloping from the sixth story to the ground, or swerve and heavily lean to keep from flying into space were his stirrup leathers not laced, and every other crucial spot of strain independent of so weak a thing as a buckle. To go up where you have come down is another and easier process for man and straps and everything, except the horse. His breath and legs are not immortal. And in order that each day the man may be hardily borne over rough and smooth he must own several mounts—a "string"; sometimes six and more, either his own property, or allotted to him by the foreman of the outfit for which he rides. The unused animals run in a herd—the ramuda; and to get a fresh mount from the ramuda means not seldom the cere-mony of catching your hare. The ponies walk sedately together in the pasture, good as gold, and eyeing you without concern until they perceive that you are come with an object. They then put forth against you all the knowledge you have bestowed upon them so painfully. They comprehend ropes and loops and the law of gravity; they have observed the errors of steers in similar cases, and the unattractive result of running inside any inclosure, such as a corral; they strategize to keep at large; and altogether, chasing a steer is tortoise play to the game they can set up for you. They relish the sight of you whirling impotent among them, rejoice in the smoking pace and the doublings they perpetrate; and with one eye attentive to you and your poised rope, and the other dex-terously commanding the universe, they will intertangle as in cross-tag, pushing between your design and its victim, mingling confusedly like a driven mist, and all this with nostrils leaning level to the wind and bellies close to the speeding ground. But when the desired one is at last taken, and your successful rope is on his neck, you would not dream he had ever wished for anything else. He stands, submitting absent-mindedly to bit and blanket, mild as any unconscious lamb, while placidity descends once more upon the herd; again they pasture good as gold, and butter would not melt in the mouth of one of these conscientious creatures. I have known a number of dogs, one crow and two monkeys, but these combined have seemed to me less fertile in expedient than the cow-pony, the sardonic cayuse. The bit his master gave him, and the bridle and spurs, have the same origin from necessity, and the same history as to ornament. If stopping and starting and turning must be like flashes of light, the apparatus is accordingly severe; and as for the spurs, those wheels with long spikes cease to seem grotesque when you learn that with shorter and sharper rowels they would catch in the corded meshes of the girth, and bring the rider to ruin. Silver and gold, when he could pay for them, went into the make and decoration of this smaller machinery; and his hat would cost him fifteen dollars, and he wore fringed gloves. His boots often cost twenty-five dollars in his brief hour of opulence. Come to town for his holiday, he wore his proud finery, and, from his wide hat-brim to his jingling heels, made something of a figure—as self-conscious and deliberate a show as any painted buck in council or bull-elk among his aspiring cows; and out of town in the mountains, as wild and lean and dangerous as buck or bull knows how to be.

As with his get-up, so it went with his vocabulary; for any manner of life with a rule and flavor of its own strong enough to put a new kind of dress on a man's body will put new speech in his mouth, and an idiom derived from the exigencies of his days and nights was soon spoken by the cow-puncher. Like all creators, he not only built, but borrowed his own wherever he found it. Chaps from *chaparajos,* is only one of many transfers from the Mexican, one out of (I should suppose) several hundred; and in lover-wolf is a singular instance of half-baked translation. *Lobo,* pronounced *lovo,* being the Spanish for wolf, and the coyote being a sort of wolf, the dialect of the southern border has slid into this name for a wolf that is larger, and a worse enemy to steers than the small coward coyote. Lover-wolf is a word anchored to its district. In the Northwest, though the same animal roams there as dangerously, his Texas name would be as unknown as the Northwest's word for Indian, "siwash," from *savage,* would be along the Rio Grande. Thus at the top and bottom of our map, the French and Spanish words trickle across the frontier, and with English melt into two separate amalgams. Other words, having the same divergent starting-points, drift everywhere, and become established in the cow-puncher's dialect over his whole country. No better French specimen can be instanced than *cache,* verb and noun, from the French verb *cacher,* to conceal. Words which have no application to permanent conditions and needs, must always pass with the generation that coined and used them, they cannot enter the polite society of the dictionary; but certain ones there are, deserving to survive; cinch, for instance from *cincha,* the Mexican girth. From its narrow office under the horse's belly it has come to perform in metaphor a hundred services. In cinching somebody or something you may mean that you hold four aces, or the key of a political crisis; and when a man is very much indeed upper-dog, then he is said to have an air-tight cinch; and this phrase is to me so pleasantly eloquent that I am withheld from using it in polite gatherings only by that prudery which we carry as a burden along with the benefits of academic training. Besides the foreign importations, such as *arroyo* and *riata,* that stand unchanged, and those others which under the action of our own speech have sloughed their native shape and come out something new, like quirt—once *cuerta,* Mexican for rawhide—is the third large class of words which the cow-boy has taken from our sober old dictionary stock and made over for himself. Pie-biter refers not to those hailing from our pie belt, but to a cow-pony who secretly forages in a camp kitchen to indulge his acquired tastes. Western whisky, besides being known as tonsil varnish and a hundred different articles, goes as benzine, not unjustly. The same knack of imagery that upon our Eastern slope gave visitors from the country the apt name of hayseed, calls their Western equivalents junipers. Hay grows scant upon the Rocky Mountains, but those seclusions are filled with evergreens. No one has accounted to me for *hobo*. A hobo is a wandering unemployed person, a stealer of rides on freight trains, a diner at the back door, eternally seeking honest work, and when brought face to face with it eternally retreating. The hobo is he against whom we have all sinned by earning our living. Perhaps some cowboy saw an Italian playing a pipe to the accompaniment of the harp, and made the generalization: oboe may have given us hobo. Hobo-ken has been suggested by an ingenious friend; but the word seems of purely Western origin, and I heard it in the West several years before it became used in the East. The cow-puncher's talent for making a useful verb out of anything shows his individuality. Any young strong race will always lay firm hands on language and squeeze juice from it; and you instantly comprehend the man who tells you of his acquaintances, whom you know to be drunk at the moment, that they are helling around town. Unsleeping need for quick thinking and doing gave these nomads the pith of utterance. They say, for instance, that they intend camping on a man's trail, meaning, concisely, "So-and-so has injured us, and we are going to follow him day and night until we are quits."

It is to be noted in all peoples that for whatever particular thing in life is of frequent and familiar practice among them they will devise many gradations of epithet. To go is in the cattle country a common act, and a man may go for different reasons, in several manners, at various speeds. For example: "Do I understand you went up the tree with the bear just behind you?"

"The bear was not in front of me."

To the several phases of going known to the pioneer as vamose, skip, light out, dust, and git, the cow-boy adds, burn the earth, hit, hit the breeze, pull your freight, jog, amble, move, pack, rattle your hocks, brindle.

It may be that some of these words I have named as home-bred natives of our wilderness are really of long standing and archaic repute, and that the scholar can point to them in the sonnets of Shakespeare, but I, at least, first learned them West of the Missouri.

With a speech and dress of his own, then, the cow-puncher drove his herds to Abilene or Westport Landing in the Texas times, and the easy abundant dollars came, and left him for spurs and bridles of barbaric decoration. Let it be remembered that the Mexican was the original cow-boy, that the American improved on him. Those were the days in which he was long in advance of settlers, and when he literally fought his right of way. Along the waste hundreds of miles that he had to journey, three sorts of inveterate enemies infested the road—the cattle and the horse thief who were as daring as himself; the supplanted Mexican, who hated the new encroaching Northern race; and the Indian, whose band was against all races but his own immediate tribe, and who flayed the feet of his captives, and made them walk so through the mountain passes to the fires in which he slowly burned them. Among these perils the cow-puncher took wild pleasure in existing. No soldier of fortune ever adventured with bolder carelessness, no fiercer blood ever stained a border. If his raids, his triumphs, and his reverses have inspired no minstrel to sing worthily of him who rode from the Pecos to the Big Horn, it is not so much the Rob Roy as the Walter Scott who is lacking. And the Flora McIvor! Alas! the stability of the clan, the blessing of the home background, was not there. These wild men sprang from the loins of no similar fathers and few begot sons to continue their hardihood. War they made in plenty, but not love; for the woman they saw was not the woman a man can take into his heart. That their fighting Saxon ancestors awoke in them for a moment and made them figures for poetry and romance is due to the strange accidents of a young country, where, while cities flourished by the coast and in the direct paths of trade, the herd-trading interior remains mediaeval in its simplicity and violence. And yet this transient generation deserves more chronicling than it will ever have. Deeds in plenty were done that are all and more than imagination should require. One high noon upon the plains by the Rio Grande the long irons lay hot in the fire. The young cattle were being branded, and the gathered herd covered the plain. Two owners claimed one animal. They talked at first quietly round the fire, then the dispute quickened. One roped the animal, throwing it to the ground to burn his mark upon it. A third came, saying the steer was his. The friends of each drew close to hear, and a claimant thrust his red hot iron against the hide of the animal tied on the ground. Another seized it from him, and as they fell struggling, their adherents flung themselves upon their horses, and massing into clans, volleyed with their guns across the fire. In a few minutes fourteen riders lay dead upon the plain, while the tied animal over which they had quarrelled bawled and bleated in the silence. Here are the makings of a ballad, but where's the maker? And once there was a certain bold man in Northern New Mexico whose war upon cattle-thieves made his life so shining a mark, that he deposited in the bank five thousand dollars to go to the man who should kill whoever killed him. A neighborhood where one looks so far beyond his own assassination as to provide a competence for his avenger, is discouraging to family life, but what a theme for a poem! Prose has been written about Billy the Kid, but that strange and desperate character should be celebrated in verse as good as Marmion.

Such existence soon makes a strange man of any one, and the early cow-punchers rapidly grew unlike all people but each other and the wild superstitious ancestors whose blood was in their veins. Their hair was often long, and their glance rested with serene penetration upon the stranger; they laughed seldom, and their spirit was in the permanent attitude of war. Grim lean men of few topics, and not many words concerning these; comprehending no middle between the poles of brutality and tenderness; indifferent to death, but disconcerted by a good woman; some with violent Old Testament religion, some avowing none, and all of them uneasy about corpses and the dark. These horsemen would dismount in camp at nightfall and lie looking at the stars, or else squat about the fire conversing with crude sombreness of brands and horses and cows, speaking of humans when they referred to men.

To-day they are still to be found in New Mexico, their last domain. The extreme barrenness of those mountains has held city and farm people at a distance. That next stage of Western progress—that unparalleled compound of new hotels, electric lights and invincible ignorance which has given us the Populist—has been retarded, and the civilization of Colorado and silver does not yet vulgarize New Mexico. But in these lean years the cow-puncher no longer can earn money to spend on ornament; he dresses poorly and wears his chaps very wide and ungainly. But he still has three mounts, with seven horses to each mount, and his life is in the saddle among vast solitudes. In the North he was a later comer, and never quite so formidable a person. By the time he had ridden up into Wyoming and Montana the Indians were mostly gone, the locomotive upon the scene, and going West far less of an exploration than it had been in Texas days. Into these new pastures drifted youths from town and country whose grit would scarcely have lasted them to Abilene, and who were not the grim long-haired type, but a sort of glorified farm-hand. They too wore their pistols, and rode gallantly, and out of them nature and simplicity did undoubtedly forge manlier, cleaner men than what our streets breed of no worse material. They galloped by the side of the older hands, and caught something of the swing and tradi-tion of first years. They developed heartiness and honesty in virtue and in vice alike. Their evil deeds were not of a sneaking kind, but had always the saving grace of courage. Their code had no place for the man who steals a pocket-book or stabs in the back.

And what has become of them? Where is this latest outcropping of the Saxon gone? Except where he lingers in the mountains of New Mexico he has been dispersed, as the elk, as the buffalo, as all wild animals must inevitably be dispersed. Three things swept him away—the exhausting of the virgin pastures, the coming of the wire fence, and Mr. Armour of Chicago, who set the price of beef to suit himself. But all this may be summed up in the word Progress. When the bankrupt cow-puncher felt Progress sinking him, he seized whatever plank floated nearest him in the wreck. He went to town for a job; he got a position on the railroad; he set up a saloon; he married, and fenced in a little farm; and he turned "rustler," and stole the cattle from the men for whom he had once worked. In these capacities you will find him to-day. The ex-cowboy who set himself to some new way of wage-earning is all over the West, and his old courage and frankness still stick to him, but his peculiar independence is of necessity dimmed. The only man who has retained this wholly is the outlaw, the horse and cattle thief, on whose grim face hostility to Progress forever sits. He has had a checkered career. He has been often hanged, often shot; he is generally "wanted" in several widely scattered districts. I know one who used to play the banjo to me on Powder River as he swung his long boots over the side of his bunk. I have never listened to any man's talk with more interest and diversion. Once he had been to Paris on the proceeds of a lengthy, well-conducted theft; once he had been in prison for murder. He had the bluest eye, the longest nose, and the coldest face I ever saw. This type of gentleman still lives and thrives in the cattle country, occasionally goes out into the waste of land in the most imperceptible way, and presently cows and steers are missed. But he has driven them many miles to avoid live-stock inspectors, and it may be that if you know him by sight and happen to be in a town where cattle are bought, such as Kansas City, you will meet him at the best hotel there, full of geniality and affluence.

Such is the story of the cow-puncher, the American descendant of Saxon ancestors, who for thirty years flourished upon our part of the earth, and, because he was not compatible with Progress, is now departed, never to return. But because Progress has just now given us the Populist and the free silverite in exchange for him, is no ground for lament. He has never made a good citizen, but only a good soldier, from his tournament days down. And if our nation in its growth have no worse distemper than the Populist to weather through, there is hope for us, even though present signs disincline us to make much noise on the Fourth of July, and ignorance may change its skin, but never dies.

Preface to *Red Men and White*

Written about the same time as "The Evolution of the Cow-Puncher," the preface to Wister's first book about the West is uncharacteristically lofty and abstract, almost Whitmanesque. Although in both essays he regards the frontier as belonging to the past, cases of individual atavism seem to interest him more than a coherent theory of racial or even of social evolution.

As in "The White Goat," Wister speaks with at least three voices: as chronicler (more than historian) of a "violent and romantic era," as regionalist, and as realist with no need "to call upon his invention."

He had noted the hypocrisy of Texans in his journal of February 22, 1893 (Owen Wister Out West, 150), and in "Skip to My Lou," published only in his last collection of Western stories, When West Was West *(Macmillan, 1928), he used the material even more scathingly.*

In his preface to the volume in the collected edition, Wister discussed the highly favorable responses to the first edition of Rudyard Kipling and Theodore Roosevelt, praised Frederic Remington's illustrations to "The Evolution of the Cow-Puncher" (the text of which is included), and quoted responses to "A Pilgrim on the Gila," the last story in the volume, which was close enough to actuality to draw outraged denials from Arizonans.

Source: Red Men and White. *(New York: Harper and Brothers, 1896.) Actually published November 8, 1895.*

THESE EIGHT STORIES are made from our Western Frontier as it was in a past as near as yesterday and almost as by-gone as the Revolution; so swiftly do we proceed. They belong to each other in a kinship of life and manners, and a little through the nearer tie of having here and there a character in common. Thus they resemble faintly the separate parts of a whole, and gain, perhaps, something of the invaluable weight of length; and they have been received by my closest friends with suspicion.

Many sorts of Americans live in America; and the Atlantic American, it is to be feared, often has a cautious and conventional imagination. In his routine he has lived unaware of the violent and romantic era in eruption upon his soil. Only the elk-hunter has at times returned with tales at which the other Atlantic Americans have deported themselves politely; and similarly, but for the assurances of Western readers, I should have come to doubt the truth of my own impressions. All this is most natural.

If you will look upon the term "United States" as describing what we are, you must put upon it a strict and Federal construction. We undoubtedly use the city of Washington for our general business office, and in the event of a foreign enemy upon our coasts we should stand bound together more stoutly than we have shown ourselves since 1776. But as we are now, seldom has a great commonwealth been seen less united in its stages of progress, more uneven in its degrees of enlightenment. Never, indeed, it would seem, have such various centuries been jostled together as they are to-day upon this continent, and within the boundaries of our nation. We have taken the ages out of their processional arrangement and set them marching disorderly abreast in our wide territory, a harlequin platoon. We citizens of the United States date our letters 18——, and speak of ourselves as living in the present era; but the accuracy of that custom depends upon where we happen to be writing. While portions of New York, Chicago, and San Francisco are of this nineteenth century, we have many ancient periods surviving among us. What do you say, for example, to the Kentucky and Tennessee mountaineers, with their vendettas of blood descending from father to son? That was once the prevailing fashion of revenge. Yet even before the day when Columbus sailed had certain communities matured beyond it. This sprout of the Middle Ages flourishes fresh and green some five hundred miles and five hundred years from New York. In the single State of Texas you will find a contrast more violent still. There, not long ago, an African was led upon a platform in a public place for people to see, and tortured slowly to death with knives and fire. To witness this scene young men and women came in crowds. It is said that the railroad ran a special train for spectators from a distance. How might that audience of Paris, Texas, appropriately date its letters? Not Anno Domini, but many years B.C. The African deserves no pity. His hideous crime was enough to drive a father to any madness, and too many such monsters have by their acts made Texas justly desperate. But for American citizens to crowd to the retribution, and look on as at a holiday show, reveals the Inquisition, the Pagans, the Stone Age, unreclaimed in our republic. On the other hand, the young men and women who will watch side by side the burning of a negro shrink from using such words as bull or stallion in polite society; many in Texas will say, instead, *male cow* and *caviard horse* (a term spelled as they pronounce it), and consider that delicacy is thus achieved. Yet in this lump Texas holds leaven as sterling as in any State; but it has far to spread.

It were easy to proceed from Maine to California instancing the remote centuries that are daily colliding within our domain, but this is enough to show how little we cohere in opinions. How many States and Territories is it that we count united under our Stars and Stripes? I know that there are some forty-five or more, and that though I belong among the original thirteen, it has been my happiness to journey in all the others, in most of them, indeed, many times, for the sake of making my country's acquaintance. With no spread-eagle brag do I gather conviction each year that we Americans, judged not hastily, are sound at heart, kind, coura-geous, often of the truest delicacy, and always ultimately of excel-lent good-sense. With such belief, or, rather, knowledge, it is sorrowful to see our fatal complacence, our as yet undisciplined folly, in sending to our State Legislatures and to that general business office of ours at Washington a herd of mismanagers that seems each year to grow more inefficient and contemptible, whether branded Republican or Democrat. But I take heart, because often and oftener I hear upon my journey the citizens high and low muttering, "There's too much politics in this country"; and we shake hands.

But all this is growing too serious for a book of short stories. They are about Indians and soldiers and events west of the Missouri. They belong to the past thirty years of our development, but you will find some of those ancient surviving centuries in them if you take my view. In certain ones the incidents, and even some of the names, are left unchanged from their original reality. The visit of Young-man-afraid-of-his-horses to the Little Big Horn and the rise and fall of the young Crow impostor, General Crook's surprise of E-egante, and many other occurrences, noble and ignoble, are told as they were told to me by those who saw them. When our national life, our own soil, is so rich in adventures to record, what need is there for one to call upon his invention save to draw, if he can, characters who shall fit these strange and dramatic scenes? One cannot improve upon such realities. If this fiction is at all faithful to the truth from which it springs, let the thanks be given to the patience and boundless hospitality of the Army friends and other friends across the Missouri who have housed my body and instructed my mind. And if the stories entertain the ignorant without grieving the judicious I am content.

Concerning the Contents

Although Wister had for some time admired Frederic Reming-
ton's work and had hoped to have him as illustrator, the two men
did not meet until September 8, 1893, in Geyser Basin, Yellow-
stone Park. Wister was delighted to discover that Remington
agreed with him "about the disgrace of our politics and the
present asphyxiation of all real love of country" (Owen Wister
Out West, 181).

This harmony of outlook persisted through the writing and
illustrating of "The Evolution of the Cow-Puncher" and beyond.
By the turn of the century, however, Remington found Wister's
stories increasingly difficult to illustrate as they became, in his
terms, less dramatic, and his last drawing for a Wister story
appeared in November 1901.

In 1897, however, the two men seemed, like Wister and the
clerk, members of the select group of those whose manhood had
been revealed in the West's silence and freedom from conventional
codes. But the unspoken code of the West is more complex than it
might seem. The clerk perceived a different West than had Wister,
and Remington transcends both visions because he is able not
only to reproduce fact but to convey truth, not only "the day-by-
day facts of the wilderness, but the eternal note also, the pity and
the awe of that epic life." Here again, Wister speaks in more than
one voice of more than one vision. With both voices he opposes
the genteel vision, oriented toward Europe, which chose to ignore
the sordid and painful facts of life. This was, of course, a side of
himself which for fifteen years he managed to suppress, rejecting it
in language drawn from artifacts of the Old World.

In addition to this preface, Wister wrote a preface and verses for Remington's A Bunch of Buckskins *(New York: R. H. Russell, 1901) and* Done in the Open *(New York: P. M. Collier and Son, 1903) which are laudatory but far less personal. See also the preface to* Members of the Family *for what amounts to a eulogy of Remington, who died in 1909.*

Ben Merchant Vorpahl's My Dear Wister—The Frederic Remington–Owen Wister Letters *(Palo Alto: American West Publishing Company, 1972), far more ambitious than the title indicates, gives an excellent account of the friendship and working relationship between the two men and an even better interpretation of it. For an interpretation of Remington as artist and writer, see Vorpahl's* Frederic Remington and the West: With the Eye of the Mind *(Austin: University of Texas Press, 1978).*

Source: Drawings of Frederic Remington *(New York: R. H. Russell, 1897).*

SOME TIME AGO I was spending a driven but happy forenoon among those shops where guns, and fishing tackle, and tents, and all the various necessities of a Western holiday are found. My time was crowded, and against the column of items on my list only a few checks had been made, when I reached "Groceries." Now, unless you have spent such forenoons and holidays yourself, the visit among the guns and fishing tackle may seem to raise questions of greater moment than any which could occur in the grocery shop. But this is not so. A man soon learns what weapons he prefers, and enters with his mind settled in advance; whereas, when it comes to evaporated vegetables, condensed soups, and pellets that can expand into a meal, you pause over each novelty, and with divided purpose wretchedly choose and unchoose until you are scarce more manlike than a woman. At least, such is my case; and having no minutes to squander this forenoon, I had penciled my supplies to avoid discussion and temptation. Even while I was directing how I wished the parcels tied, mentioning that they were to be much jolted on the backs of horses, the shopman looked suddenly alert, and said this sounded like a camping trip. Yes, I told him in my elation, I was bound for the head waters of Wind River in Wyoming. Instantly the merchant fell from him; every trace of groceries left his expression; his eye beamed with eagerness, and he asked in the voice of one who gives the countersign, "Have you ever been to Arizona?" and hearing that I had, "I served there under Crook!" he exclaimed. Then names of the North and South came to his lips—San Carlos, San Simon, the Gila, the Chiricahuas, the Tonto Basin, the forks of the Owyhee, Boisé, Bidwell, Harney—he spoke of many familiar to me; and next we were hard at it, this old soldier and myself, exchanging enthusiasms, gossiping in comradeship among the dried prunes. Thus I wasted minutes that I could not spare, yet lost nothing by it; my parcels were put up right. And when this errand was finished, he watched me depart from the shop door, and signed, "I should like to see it all again!"

Since that day I have gone back to him, not always to buy groceries, but just to pass the word, and thus in the midst of city streets to conjure up Arizona, or Idaho, or Wyoming. My journeys through those regions have come after his time. I know none of his dangers and not many of his hardships. But I too have seen Summer and Winter in the Rocky Mountains, and the sun rise; and have slept and marched on trails where he went once. Between us is established a freemasonry: both of us have been *out there;* both of us understand. It matters not that one was an enlisted man campaigning against Indians, while the other is nothing but a voluntary pilgrim to the wilderness. Upon both alike has the wilderness set its spell. Yes; we certainly understand.

And what is this spell? Scarcely danger, for I have met no dangers worthy of the name. Scarcely freedom, since the enlisted man can do by no means what he pleases. Scarcely the immortal lift and purity of that great air, which I feel, indeed, but to which I can not remember hearing any trooper allude. Neither will the splendor of Nature explain it; the inspiring vastness, the transfigurations of the sunset, the swimming oceans of color, rich, subtle, endless, the more inexhaustible as the more observed.

Only the pilgrims value these things. The chance for riches it certainly is not, nor the chance for crime. Crime and Fortune are there as everywhere; but the lost pocketbook is returned when it would not be in a city, and you meet with few that are troubling about dollars. Bloody and sudden as death often is there, it is not the planned murder so much as the quick blow of personal vengeance, the primitive man dealing with his fellow as in justice he expects his fellow will deal with him. Finally, it is not adventure alone. Though roving spirits have come to their own upon the plains, and with Indians and cattle-driving have let loose the fervid energy no town gave room for, dreamers strayed there too, many dreamers, and found happiness. In all of this I am speaking of the wilderness as it was once, and almost is no more. But you will find the dreamers still, now and then, riding alone from horizon to horizon, paddling upon sequestered rivers, hermiting in quiet cabins, all of them escaped from social codes, reaping the reward and paying the penalty in that archaic silence. For indeed the silence of that world seems to have come unbroken from behind Genesis, to have been earlier than the beginning, to make one with the planets, to have known mysteries, that dwindle Rome to a show. The little sounds of earth do not break it. In it the painted Indian walks naked, the twin of its mystery. In it you can wake or sleep, and no man hinders. Whatever law there is rises from the ground or falls from the stars. For the very living, life seems to mingle with the origin before the dust has returned to dust. That is the spell for trooper or for pilgrim. From empire to empire, our wise brains have devised conventions that we may live together, but our unwise hearts crave the something that wisdom has renounced for us. So most of those you will meet in the wilderness, be they doers or dreamers, have followed the heart's desire and escaped back to Nature.

Ah, there is a lotus also in the West! It has drugged many that have never returned. But if you wisely tear yourself from it and re-enter the fold of civilization, and in respectable content sell groceries, for instance, your heart will remind you of *out there*, now and then, a word like Owyhee or Wind River will give you a homesickness for the nameless magic of the plains.

Those happy ones who have known it meet always in that freemasonry which set the soldier and me talking like old acquaintances. And therefore I am going to show him these drawings; for every one will speak to him of *out there*. He will rejoice in their truth—indeed truth is a pale word—it is the vibrating thing itself which seems to rise out of these pages. Even to me they flash and throb with life I have lived, and how much more to a man whose years preceded mine and who had dangers where I had none!

I have stood before many paintings of the West. Paintings of mountains, paintings of buffalo, paintings of Indians—the whole mystic and heroic pageant of our American soil; the only great romantic thing our generation has known, the last greatly romantic thing our Continent holds; indeed the poetic episode most deeply native that we possess. And now I have seen for myself, and know how he has caught alive not only the roped calf, or the troop cook sucking his comfortable corn-cob, the day-by-day facts of the wilderness, but the eternal note also, the pity and the awe of that epic life. He has made them visible by his art, and set them down as a national treasure. Look at the Pony War Dance. That wild fury of religion, that splendor of savagery clashes down to us from the Stone Age. If you will open the Old Testament where Joshua delayed the course of the sun, or they blew down a city wall with a trumpet, you will come upon the same spirit. Look at the Medicine-men and the lightning. Again man's untamed original soul communes with a God of vengeance and terror. Is it not like Elijah and the fire-stroke from heaven upon the altar? Then turn to the Sheep-herder's breakfast. Unless you have known that solitude, no words of mine can tell you how Remington has been a poet here. With some lines and smears on paper he has expressed that lotus mystery of the wilderness. He has taken a ragged vagrant with a frying-pan and connected him with the eternal. The dog, the pack-saddle, the ass, the dim sheep in the plain, those tender outlines of bluffs and ridges—it is Homer or the Old Testament again; time and the present world have no part here!

Perhaps you do not value all this as I do. Perhaps the seamy side shuts you from the rest, and you shrink from the brutality of man and the suffering of beast. I have heard people speak thus sometimes, and give thanks for their books, and their bathrooms, for the opera, and for Europe where they can travel in a landscape seasoned by history. Well, Europe is richer, much richer, than any desert, and it is toward its use and comprehension, on the whole, that our struggling faces are set. Our fond, quack-ridden Republic looks, after all, toward the old world for its teaching. But we have a landscape seasoned by mystery, where chiefs and heroes move, fit subjects for the poet. If you do not see this, perhaps you are too near. Let me ask you to think of the bloody slaughters in Homer, and of all the great art you know from him to the present day; has not the terrible its share of notice? Doubtless you would have stopped Homer's reciting to you how bodies were hacked to pieces beneath the walls of Troy, and how swinish were sometimes the companions of Ulysses. But now you read it all with pleasure. Do you believe Art would have amounted to much if it had excluded pain and ugliness and narrowed its gaze upon the beautiful alone?

At any rate I am glad that we have Remington, one of the kind that makes us aware of things we could not have seen for ourselves. We have been scarce enough in native material for Art to let go what the soil provides us. We have often failed to value what the intelligent foreigner seizes upon at once. And I think as the Frontier recedes into tradition, fewer of us will shrink from its details. If Remington did nothing further, already has he achieved: he has made a page of American history his own.

Autumn on Wind River

This poem, a fair if not an inspiring example of Wister's poetic efforts, reveals a good deal about his literary roots in genteel romanticism in its use of personification and pastel language. His prose work began in the same kind of diction and vision, but direct observation sometimes resulted in more straightforward and realistic language.

With minor variants in accidentals and a substitution of "cotton-woods' leafless ranks" for "cottonwoods' ghost-ranks" in line 9, the poem was published as "In the After-Days" at the conclusion of Lin McLean.

Source: Harper's Monthly 94 (April 1897): 774.

The black pines stand high up the hills,
    The white snow sifts their columns deep,
While through the cañon's riven cleft
    From there, beyond, the rose clouds sweep.

Serene above their paling shapes
    One star hath wakened in the sky,
And here in the gray world below
    Over the sage the wind blows by,

Rides through the cottonwoods' ghost-ranks,
    And hums aloft a sturdy tune
Among the river's tawny bluffs,
    Untenanted as is the moon.

Far 'neath the huge invading dusk
    Comes Silence awful through the plain;
But yonder horseman's heart is gay,
    And he goes singing might and main.

Educating the Polo Pony

The material for this essay apparently came from Wister's trip to Texas in February and March 1893, when he visited the ranch of Fitzhugh Savage near Brownwood. The diary entries in Owen Wister Out West *contain no mention of polo ponies nor much description of the countryside.*

In this essay, there is a sharp split between the description of the journey to find the pony, done in the style of southwestern humorists, and the narrative of the pony's training. The first style is colloquial; the joke is on the teller. The second style is more formal, and in the assumption that a pony can, like a common soldier, rise through the ranks, become socially more acceptable, there is a condescension wider and deeper than mere anthropomorphism. The implication, though it runs counter to most of Wister's conscious pronouncements in the 1890s, is that Newport is better than Texas and that civilized restraint is preferable to natural wilderness. However, as Mark Twain said of Fenimore Cooper, Wister is often more interesting when he is not noticing than when he is.

For the tenderfoot rider's view of polo, emphasizing his ignorance and ineptitude, see Wister's "How They Taught Me Polo," Harper's Weekly *39 (April 6, 1895): 334.*

Source: Outing *36 (June 1900): 296–99. Four photographs included.*

WE MUST remain uncertain whether the polo pony moralizes upon the variableness of life or takes his destiny and his meals unthinkingly. No other animal meets with more chances, or treads wider ground for reflection. Not another of the creatures fallen into the domesticating company of man ends further from his beginnings. In unroofed, unlimited Texas, houseless, unfed, ungroomed, with a long mane and a flowing tail, he is suddenly picked and promoted from the ranks, given corn and bran and sugar-cane, educated like a specialist, and watched like an heir apparent. Presently he enters Newport, roached and docked, to live in a stable, and manœuvre in the eye of fashion, having ascended through the steepest contrasts of experience. Very few of the families that buy him have seen themselves rise more abruptly.

It would embarrass him to find you his parents. Yet they, likely enough, are still running about as usual in happy Texas, with a long mane and a flowing tail, unconscious of the progress of their child, and begetting younger brothers to follow in his steps. Possibly the only thing he finds at Newport to remind him of his old cow-punching days is the language spoken by his riders upon occasions during their game.

For it is upon somebody's ranch that he made his beginning—let us say in McCulloch County, or San Saba. If he has seen fences they have been of barbed wire, and somewhat longer than the fences in Rhode Island. There is a certain fenced pasture in McCulloch County called the "small pasture." It is nine miles square. If he has seen grass—but the notion is preposterous. Go yourself and look at McCulloch County or San Saba. You will see a world as bald as the moon, stretching naked to the Pacific. This world has the skin on in Texas; when it gets to Arizona it has only bones. Or you will see, southward and eastward, perhaps, a thick, gray thatched hairy hide of thorns clothing the world; they are knee-deep and wicked; and if a pony chewed them, glass bottles would be good enough for him in Newport, and make him fat. Then there are cactus and the smoke-weed. Also, here and there, you will come upon miles of apparent orchards and a rural neighborhood, so evenly do the trees seem planted, and so much do they resemble peach and apple trees. But the apple are only live-oak; the peach are only mesquite; there is no rural neighborhood; and the orchard wall and the white steeple that you cannot help expecting just over the next hill, never turn up. You may see a wolf, and beyond him the rest of Texas.

This is the world as the polo pony has known it before civilization laid its selecting hand upon him. And what he would call grass is a flickering ghostly yellow appearance, which an Eastern horse could not detect with the naked eye. Then comes his day. Perhaps he has been the sole possession of a cow-puncher, who parts with him for double or treble the price that he paid. A few years ago that would be, say, thirty dollars, or even forty, if the pony were of great promise. But polo has grown a sport so active (and certainly it is the very emperor of games!) that even in distant Texas must civilization get up earlier in the morning and hunt farther afield for the raw material from which it is to manufacture the ultimate Newport standard article.

The call for ponies in the East has come to be heard widely in the West, and the cow-puncher who would part with his little horse for thirty dollars (and often much less) seven or eight years ago will not do so to-day. The industry has become recognized. It has been rumored that a certain pony which so-and-so sold to what's-his-name for twenty-five dollars in San Saba was taken to Dedham, or Radnor, or Ipswich, or Woodsburg, and sold for six hundred. The improvements that were built by the middleman upon the pony between these two transactions are not taken wholly into account by the Texas mind; therefore, does the raw material come higher to-day.

But in 1893 the middleman did not have either to pay so much or to cover so many hundreds of miles to procure the horses that he needed. The gathering was done nearer his headquarters, nearer the home pasture, and the training ground, and the feeding corral. Sometimes a pony would fairly drop out of the sky for him. He would be going about some other business; he would meet a citizen jogging along the road, and instantly discern that he wanted the citizen's mount, subject of course to certain conditions. The pony was not more than five, was he? Six? Well, that was pretty old for a horse to begin learning a new trade. Pretty old, did you say? Why, that horse was so smart you'd find him learning new trades at twelve. Looking for something speedy? Here it was. Fifty witnesses could testify as to that. In search of a roping horse? This one could turn on a half-dollar. Well, how high was he? Fourteen-one? Just exactly. Well, maybe he might be suitable as to size, but he was spoiled because they had raced him. No, sir, they'd never raced him. Just tried him behind the barn. Fifty witnesses could testify, etc., etc.; and in a few more minutes the two have reached the county seat, and the pony has been measured and sold for fifteen dollars, and next week turns out to be a prize for nerve and sense and agility. And even while he was being measured and more words about fifty witnesses were freely flowing—lo! another pony is observed tied in front of the saloon, and (to make it short) he's now eating a pensioner's oats in a Pennsylvania home.

It was not always so easy, even in 1893. Imagine to yourself a little talk at headquarters, of this sort.

There's a man at Voca says he has a horse. (Voca was a place, half a day's ride, and it was pronounced Bokay, partly for Spanish reasons.)

What does he say it's like? Says he thinks we'll want it. Says if we do, we'll have to come for it. He's busy working off his road-tax. How do you find him? Over by the three-cornered school-house. Name's Brown.

This geography and identification seem enough, and an early morning start is made. The road turns away from the ranch and the open country of live-oak around it, across several barbed-wire fences, where you lay the panels down. Then you come into the hide of thorns, and the Spanish oaks, and the post-oaks, and the black oaks, and the scrub-oaks; and unless you are a botanist of parts, it may be doubted if you will notice anything deeper about these varieties than their spikes. You pass this lonely and intricate wilderness—intricate from its unbroken similarity, and its number of similar trails—and come down into a new, open country of stones and sand, and perhaps some cactus, and then a stream with pecan trees and a store, where nobody ever heard of the three-cornered school-house.

Yes, somebody comes in and does know all about it. You are to go that road, three miles, and turn to the left. And he points for you. At the end of three miles there is nothing. But at the end of four there is a man, sitting on a stump. Mr. Brown live near here? He thinks for a very long while, and then tells you there is no Brown, that the nearest man this way is Mr. Williams. To the right. Seven miles. Near the three-cornered school-house? No. That's to the left. Not far. A short six miles from where we are standing. There is a man lives round there somewhere, and there's no reason his name should not be Brown. Never knowed what it was. Shouldn't be surprised to hear it was Brown.

We leave the man on the stump, and, after a mile or so along the left-hand road, an old lady in a buggy tells us that she guesses what we mean *ought to be* just about ten minutes the other side of those trees. What she meant by *ought to be* can never be known. Beyond the trees was a small and humble tenement, with another lady who was feeding pigs. Three-cornered schoolhouse? She didn't know it. She hadn't lived here very long. There was a school-house burned down somewhere here once. But that was before she moved into the county. Never heard anybody say it was three-cornered. Did we mean the Red Creek school-house? If we did, we must have passed right by that, about five miles back. Mr. Brown? Oh, yes. He was working off his roadtax this week. He lived just behind the Red Creek school-house.

At three in the afternoon, having begun at seven, we found this hateful building, and Mr. Brown's wife in the vicinity. Brown was not there. But the horse was, and if we would come with her———. We did go with her. The horse was a piebald arrangement with no eyelashes and long teeth, plainly starved from inability to chew. She told us it was a colt. We never knew what Brown would have told us.

But things must not be made out worse than their actuality. Upon our journey back, we met the man on the stump. He was now riding on a very decent pony.

Find that three-cornered school-house? Well, I guessed you wouldn't. Guess you did find Brown. I could have told you all about him. Didn't know you was inquiring for *that* Brown. Now, if you was in search of a horse———

So we reached headquarters long after dark, but not empty-handed. That pony turned out well also, beginning his strange education the next day by hearing what his brothers before him in the herd might have to tell him severally of their own experience.

How they had been roping ponies for a while, but not too long to injure their speed. How the ground stuff that was liberally fed to them out of a machine which went round and round in the center of the corral more than compensated for the loss of their manes, and the painful trials of docking. How you mustn't mind if your tail did quiver eccentrically for a long while after the operation. How the bits were not so severe as some they had known in the days when they cut out cattle from the bunch. How you could run loose in the pasture during free hours, and kick and bite your enemies just as well as you ever did.

How there seems to be a sort of people living here or gathering here from elsewhere, who are quite certainly demented. How they attach the greatest importance to a detestable little white ball, and ride you after it, and express the strongest opinions about each other during the process.

It is to be supposed that the newcomer among the ponies, just as the new boy at school, must hear things of this sort in some language from his more initiated companions, and that very likely they endeavor to appal him with the grossest exaggerations concerning the day's work. His own work will probably begin with certain trials of his mouth, and his eye, and his speed. He will be ridden about rapidly with perhaps a rope, and turned suddenly, or hauled up short.

Presently his rider will make him familiar with the implements of the strange game, riding him at all speeds and in all directions, and at the same time whirling the mallet round and round, or striking the ball forward, back, and at all angles.

Then as the weeks go on, and November has changed to February, the new pony will be himself well initiated. He will have become, in proportion to his native cleverness, almost as hot over the contest as the rider, whom he judged to be crazy at the start. There, in the midst of that singular landscape, with the live-oaks making you think of apples in New England, and the mesquite producing a cheating picture of Delaware peach orchards, while in reality such things are a good eight days' journey distant, he matures in his knowledge of polo until, about the end of March, he is ready to leave the land of his birth and take that eight days' journey and arrive where there are real peach trees and real apples; though it is not likely that he will have much chance to notice them. Possibly he will become quite famous. Certainly, as was said at the beginning, no animal can have more reasons for appreciating the inequalities of life. It is to be trusted that in Newport he does not entirely forget that he was once a plain American pony: one of the people; a son of the soil.

Concerning "Bad Men"

Wister's essays usually have a clear context; this one is almost unique in having none. The commentators do not so much as mention it. Although it obviously is based on conclusions which Wister drew about the West, it draws on no identifiable experience. Wister may have been thinking back to the character of Dean Drake or formulating the distinction between "a dangerous man" and "a brave man," including the idea that a coward will "always go to shooting before it's necessary," which he states in Chapter Three of The Virginian. *However, he apparently did not write this part of the novel until early in 1902.*

The essay itself has elements common to much of Wister's work. There is the (perhaps unconscious) condescension in the notion that the boy, blessed with a good heart, could have been (at best?) a Wells, Fargo shotgun rider. There is the belief that, in evolutionary terms, the frontier is "a modern moment of an earlier universal epoch" and that, in psychological terms, it is "just ourselves expressed in unbridled terms. . . ." In other words, societies develop; individuals do not. The West may become civilized by eastern standards; human beings are unchangeable.

Relatively new, however, are Wister's attempts to point out an overt moral and to define the perfect type of human being who is bound not, as all three anecdotes indicate, by social law but by individual virtue. Right action—and this is also true of The Virginian *as it had not been of* Lin McLean—*is always chivalric action. He is also more alert than he had been in the 1890s to the differences between life as observed (or, in these cases, reported) and life as portrayed in fiction, between what would make a*

conventionally "good story" and what is true to human nature, not just in the realistic period but in all great literature. Perhaps his aesthetic was closer to that of Frank Norris (see "A Plea for Romantic Fiction") than to that of more publicly acknowledged masters like William Dean Howells and Henry James.
    Source: Everybody's 4 *(April 1901): 320–26.*

A STRIPLING OF effeminate rosiness and neat attire sat in the corner of a frontier saloon, modest, silent, and as far out of the way as he could get. He had stepped from the train, and he was waiting for the stage. It was starched linen that he wore; the city showed quite plainly in his hat; and it is still in dispute whether any down was visible upon his lip. But he was old enough to be smoking a cigar with all the appearance of habit. This cigar, also, was not a native of the town. In fact, the young man had made no purchase upon entering the saloon; nevertheless, the proprietor could scarcely complain of him. The stranger had asked if he might wait here for the stage, and had thanked the proprietor for his permission.

Then he had sought his quiet corner, and lighted his cigar.

That was all. It seems harmless and proper conduct, does it not? You would not say that there was anything here to invite calamity: what offence had the youth given?

His trouble was that he had come to the wrong place. There are parts of the world where not to be indigenous constitutes in itself an offence; and this town was one of them. Of course nobody had been born there yet—no grown-up person, that is—and therefore you might say that nobody was indigenous. But there are also parts of the world where you can become indigenous in fifteen minutes; only this poor youth had no chance. Nor had he any wish save to sit in his inconspicuous corner and smoke his cigar in peace. With his neat clothes, however, and his white shirt, there could be no inconspicuousness in that town.

A citizen walked out of the back room and up to the bar. He had left a faro game; and the proprietor was friendly with him, but respectful: that sort of respect which is flavored delicately with just enough familiarity to bring it out. It is probable that the citizen had had more drinks than the one he now took. It is also likely that faro had not gone as well with him this morning as he considered his due. His dissatisfied eye fell upon the rosy youth and his cigar; and he took the glass from his lips and held it, considering the stranger.

At length, without removing his eyes, he inquired: "What Christmas tree did that drop off of?"

The proprietor hastened to take this view. "Its express-tag has fluttered away, I guess," he whispered, jocosely.

The citizen remembered his whiskey, swallowed it, set the glass gently down, gently drew his six-shooter, and shot the cigar to smash out of the young man's mouth.

Now I do not at all know what I should have done in the young man's place. Something sensible, I hope. What the youth did I know I should not have done. You will see that his behavior was out of the common. He stooped down, picked up his cigar, found it ruined, put it in the spittoon, got a fresh one out of his pocket, found a match in his waistcoat, slid it along the seat of his nice breeches, lighted the new cigar, and settled himself once more in his chair, without a word of protest, or an attempt at resentment. The proprietor saw him do it all, and told about it afterwards.

The citizen took the second cigar, smash! like the first. Perhaps he went a trifle nearer the youth's lip.

What were the card players in the back room doing at all this noise? They all lay flat on the floor like the well-trained, indigenous people that they were, minding their own business. For there was no rear exit.

The youth felt in his waistcoat pocket, but brought no match from it. So he rose with still another fresh cigar in his hand, and walked to the bar.

"I'll have to ask you for a match," he said to the proprietor, who at once accommodated him.

Once again he slid the match beneath his coat-tails, and bringing up his own six-shooter, shot the citizen as instantly dead as that can be done.

When the young man came for the match, I wanted to make him ask, not the proprietor but the citizen for it. You can see for yourself how thrilling it would be to have the citizen made the innocent contributor to his own destruction. That slight change would have made a fine, flagrant, unlikely thing out of it, good enough for a play. And it would be easy enough now to run on and pretend, say, that the proprietor immediately pushed the bottle of whiskey and the box of cigars towards the youth, urged him to help himself freely, loaded him with congratulations, told him that he had been just going to kill the deceased himself, because deceased was an outrage on the face of the earth, and the town had got tired of him. While this was going on, the town could gradually rise in instalments from the floor, and come in and get used to the news, and begin to remember things just like this that happened to it during the John Day excitement, or when it was prospecting on the Pecos, or raising prunes in the Big Bend, or, in short, practising any of its several previous industries. Then the stage could drive up, and the young man could get in and go away; and just as it was occurring to everybody that they would like to know his name and occupation, a dark-eyed girl could break through and fling herself upon the corpse with cries of love and vengeance. Or, if you please, the proprietor could fly from the saloon calling, "Murder!" and in two minutes we could have the doors barred and the young man standing a siege in the front room. Oh, yes, various sets of sequences might follow this beginning, and each of them be fair enough in the way of probability. But that is not the point.

The above incident is a fact, or was repeated as a fact to several people who found no reason to doubt it. If invented, it is invented along lines so characteristic of frontier possibility that its weak spots are no weaker than in hundreds and thousands of actual occurrences. It needs no sequel, to my thinking, to make it of complete interest. It stands independent upon its own legs, because it reveals some human nature.

Let us pick it all to pieces and see what we can find.

There's nothing significant until the first shot. The saloon is ordinary. The proprietor is ordinary, the displeasure of the citizen at the stranger's appearance is ordinary. As for that appearance, the stranger might have been wearing good clothes for half a dozen ordinary reasons—ignorance, vanity, intentional disguise, or because he had been travelling in Pullman cars, and was waiting to unpack and put on garments more fitting to his surroundings. You can get nothing from any of this, unless that the citizen judged too easily by appearances. Even the firing of the shot has been done by too many different kinds of men to tell us which kind this one was.

But the shot hits the cigar. That is not a fluke. If it had been a fluke, the marksman might have pretended it wasn't and looked indifferent about it; but the proprietor, as you have seen, was the calibre of man to give it away at once. Under the shock of the surprise he would have done something, or said something. But he was not surprised. So the citizen is evidently a good shot, and known to be so. This is our first significant fact.

Now we come to the boy.

You can be sure that he instantly drew the same important inference that it was no blunderer who had shot his cigar out of his mouth. In the light of his whole conduct it is plain that he was gifted not only with impregnable coolness, but with an enviably prompt and perfect mind. He could judge people at sight. You see, if he had thought that first shot a fluke, he would never have given the citizen the chance to aim at a second cigar and—deplore the unfortunate consequences. If there was to be a funeral, he proposed to select the corpse himself. So sitting in his old position with a new cigar in his mouth was not such a tempting of Providence as it looks. They say. "Know yourself"; I say, "Know your man." The other may be the root of wisdom, but don't you think this is undoubtedly the apple?

There is some very bad tempting of Providence in the next move of the adventure. Why on earth, after such an exhibition of nerve as the apparent tenderfoot had given, did the citizen try it again? We cannot follow the working of the citizen's mind with any certainty, because it was not a good mind. If a man's brain is inferior, it is like any imperfect instrument, like a watch that loses or gains: it is only of the perfect watch that you can be sure it will point to twelve when twelve is the hour. The citizen's whole performance looks like that of a man who has not even intellect enough to observe inaccurately. And we can be sure that he was not a nice man. You yourself would have been won over by such gallant reception of your onslaught.

That brings us to the second shot.

It was as good as the other. The boy now had a proof of his first conclusion, that the citizen knew how to shoot. For the same reasons that we know it, he also must have now known that the citizen was a fool. The nature of the citizen's heart did not probably interest him; but at this repetition of the insult, he must have become four or forty times more deadly in every fibre and molecule of his being. The only thing we can't be quite sure of is, did he intend to kill the citizen from the start? Might he merely have plotted to "get the drop" on the citizen, and then take a revenge more playful? I'm sorry I can't work this out. But everything else goes as straight as a demonstration in geometry. His plan sprang whole to life in his brain almost with the first pistol flash. It may be that in picking up his cigar, examining its ruin, and dropping it into the spittoon, he was giving his critical faculty time to run over the work his creative faculty had just struck off; but you see that couldn't take long; he mustn't be suspiciously deliberate; the citizen was watching him, with a weapon already drawn; and at this stage he could not be sure how much of a fool the citizen was, but only that he was a good shot. So a minute, or less, finds him sliding that match along the seat of his breeches, with his plan endorsed by his critical faculty, and already in operation. It wouldn't have done at all, you see, for him to walk up at once and play this match-striking game with the proprietor, for that might have been seen through. No: he must establish this match-striking as a line of harmless conduct in the minds of the others, and under its cover strike his blow. So he submitted to having his cigar shot at again. It was very masterly. And it does look a little as if he had intended death from the first; but we can be certain only that he did intend it now. So should I; and so would you, I believe. You may not like to acknowledge yourself capable of killing a man by so coldly reasoned a process. But it was only the youth's reason that remained cold, you may be sure; another proof of its splendid quality. Most of us, if we were not by this time clammy and limp with fright, and our reason clammy and limp like the rest of our system, and therefore useless, would be a great deal hotter than white-hot with rage, and our reason would be hot like that, too, and therefore just as useless as if it were clammy and limp; so that we should do something blind and foolish. But this boy's reason was as unshaken by the transient passions of his body as is the law of gravity by the east and west wind. He was in an implacable fury, and it did not move him a hair's breadth. So he goes on with his plan. He gets out a fresh cigar. He feels for another match. The other man is doing just what he wanted him to. If he was in the habit of feeling intellectual joy, these moments must have been great pleasure to him. Then he walks up to the bar and makes his request of the proprietor.

We must go back to the citizen now.

Conceive of his standing idle while a rosy-cheeked stripling in a starched shirt, whom he had taken to be a sort of fragile, inexperienced orchid, behaved himself like this. Would not such a portent have set you thinking?

Walk into any piano shop. After the dampers have been lifted from the wires of the pianos, let somebody strike a bass note on one of them, and then listen how its neighbors hum and echo to that sound in their sensitive insides. We are like musical instruments in one another's presence. When the dampers are lifted, if any note is struck, that corresponding note vibrates in us also if we possess it. If it's a brain note, people call us wide awake, and if it's a heart note they call us sympathetic. Now the citizen stood in the neighborhood of a brain that was going like a dynamo; and his own brain ought to have buzzed busily in response. There's no question of dampers here: everybody was attentive. But the citizen had no brain that could buzz.

And how about his heart? Why, that was dumb and despicable, too! If it had contained a spark of generosity or a fibre of real courage, it would have warmed up surely now. Its courage would have vibrated and answered to the courage in the boy. The citizen would have dropped his persecuting and have become a brother.

He might have said something of this sort: "Friend, you have me beat. There's my gun. Don't do anything to me. You're the best thing I've seen in this country, and I ain't worth your powder." That would be a pleasant story, true to the best in the heart of man, and sure to bring down both gallery and boxes. It has often been a temptation to tell it thus. But you'll agree that such facts are far better left as life gave them. Romance shall not decorate that citizen. He was stirred by no appeal, intellectual or human. His nature stuck in the mud. He was in truth an ugly beast, and we need not be sorry for him at all.

We get a side light on the proprietor in his handing the boy the match so immediately. I think the proprietor had become frightened. The proprietor had some brains, or he would not have been running a successful saloon.

And here let us criticise the story's weak point. It is not the boy. Brain power of his kind found a wide arena and a ready market on the frontier, both on the side of law and order and against them. The boy was an old head with a young face. It is the citizen whose excellent shooting and dense brain do not match well. Good shots are apt to have sharp wits. Still, these sharp wits need not be observant of character. They may be only good judges of distance. We must suppose—and it is not difficult or improbable—that the citizen's brain all went to target practice and showing off; this very cigar-shooting may have been partly to exact his tribute of admiration from the latest arrival. The citizen is not hard to swallow when he is explained. His skill and his stupidity were like a team that will not pull together, and they wrecked the vehicle to which inscrutable nature had harnessed them.

Now the youth places that last match behind his hip, as if to light it as he had lighted its predecessor.

You will notice that his plan of attack bears the final test of perfection: it can be abandoned at any moment that the enemy, or circumstances, make this advisable. Should the citizen become suspicious and cover the boy with his weapon, all the boy has to do is simply to go and light the match. He will have committed himself to nothing, and have revealed nothing. It is a very fine plan.

But the citizen stands innocent and utterly hoodwinked, and the boy's triumphant hand lays hold of his pistol. He knows that his game is won and that he has the citizen at his mercy. At his mercy? In you and in me and in most people, surely it would be so. By this time the rage in us that meant killing would have had time to cool down to that point where true proportions rise again into sight, and it would have come home to us that, after all, the tormentor did not deserve destruction; any amount of humiliation, any amount of brutal horse-play you please, but not destruction. Cover him with your pistol, show him up to the bystanders, tell him in their presence what you think of him with every term of vitriolic ridicule that your invention can devise; or, do it the other way; compliment his marksmanship and apologize for having deceived him by your appearance; admit that you were culpable in coming to town dressed in such a way, and invite him to drink with you. Why, the very pleasure of your triumph would have helped to make you merciful, if not good-humored. But mercy was not in the boy's make-up; so he shot the citizen dead.

Through that act we reach the final piece of knowledge in this enlightening story.

That the citizen's was not a life worth preserving has nothing to do with the heart of the boy. He had as bad a heart, and as cold, I think, as is humanly possible. Sometimes, though rarely, it seems as if nature attempted to produce a pure Satan, a Satan unmixed and flawless; and specimens like this boy come very near to what are called in business contracts the specifications. In fiction it is not well to have many such perfectly symmetrical characters; characters where no counter impulses of goodness defeat the main design; for though such natures are occasional facts, they lie outside the general outline of truth. Shakespeare has given us but one. But as a fact, such a boy as this is valuable in an examination of the true nature of the "bad" man; and here for a while we will leave him and look at another case.

This next story is also true, and it comes much closer to the writer's personal experience. He was not present during any part of it, but he was not far off; and one of the chief actors narrated to him the whole occurrence.

A doctor was sent for to a ranch some twenty miles from the town where he had established his office. The round-up was hard by at the time, and the doctor slept in the bunk-house, which was full of highly animated cow-punchers. These indulged in some athletic scuffling, and one puncher, perfectly friendly, hit the doctor with a pillow. The doctor, equally in joke, sprang up and threw him. A bout, half of wrestling and half of sparring and also perfectly friendly, followed on this, and the doctor easily had the best of it. For, besides being probably quite as muscular as the cowboy, he had science to help him. But he was new in the country, and did not observe what was happening. During their scuffle round the room, as they were passing the puncher's bed, the man seized up his pistol from it. But another cowboy caught his hand in time, and the bullet went into the floor by the doctor's feet. This was the first intimation which the doctor had that he and sudden death were sporting together. The play, which with him had gone on as it began, innocent and good-humored, had progressed into earnest, and then into a wild intent to kill, in the cow-puncher. All of us have seen sparring matches where temper has been lost and the true game a little forgotten; but few, I imagine, have seen anything like this. The doctor had a sensation. After a little while, when the cowboy became cool again, he was very sorry—honestly sorry. He asked to shake hands, and owned that he had been "hasty." And so in time they all went to sleep, as innocent and satisfied as children; and next morning the cow-puncher rode off early to town to get his mail.

If this story ended here, perhaps it would not have been worth telling. But it does not end here.

Town was also the doctor's destination this morning, and in due time he arrived there. Entering his office, a not unusual thing awaited him a corpse laid out. In this town they always brought dead people to the doctor's room. He inquired who this was, for the head had been shot beyond identification. It was the cow-puncher; and they told him what had happened. The man had ridden into town, got his mail, taken it to the room of a girl where he always stayed when he came to town, read his letter there, and shot himself on finishing it. They never knew why. He had torn the letter into scraps.

The lesson given to the doctor by such an experience was this: never play with people who care nothing for their own lives. They may not care for yours.

But the story teaches other things. You will readily see how tempting are these facts to make fiction from. Here was this cow-puncher—this poor, unhappy fellow, as he will always seem to me riding about the sage-brush, roping cattle, living along like his lusty, careless brothers, with something steadily eating his heart out and steadily killing his mind all the while. If you pause and think of him, keeping up appearances day after day in that huge rough world of space and sunshine and hilarity, hail-fellow-well-met with his companions day and night, yet really shut up in a black box with his misery, really lonely and gradually drowning, with no one to help him swim, in a life that was too much for him, is it not a tragedy? You wonder what the whole story could have been, and imagination sets to work. But these few raw facts are better left alone. As he stands, with one day of his life glaring to the sight and all the rest veiled, this cowboy is more striking as a piece of actuality than he could ever be in romance. Indeed, had I ventured to put him in romance, do you know what would have happened? You would have laid the story down wearily, and said how you wished that these dime-novelists would now and then tell you something you could believe, instead of insulting your intelligence with stagey impossibilities. And you would have been right. Truth is never stranger than fiction; but fact often is: many facts would be entirely impossible if they had not happened. These have no business in fiction.

And now, about the cow-puncher. Was he a "bad" man? You know he was not. Yet he tried to kill a man who was playing with him. He tried to do exactly what the other boy did do and with far less provacation. No one had shot cigars out of his mouth. Concrete death, concrete murder, substantive crime would have resulted from his act, just as it did from the other. Let us see this clearly. Suppose his pistol had not been diverted, and he had killed the doctor—a very valuable life in the community. Naturally they would have taken him prisoner in the bunk-house, and thence to justice, let us suppose. The plea of self-defense would have been false. The plea of insanity hard to establish. The plea of "hasty," his own apology, would have been the only true one, and in that country it might have been sufficient to save him from hanging. But he would have had—if law were not defeated—a heavy sentence, and have gone to prison. Yet, knowing everything, do you think prison was the right place for him? Personally I do not—nor an insane asylum either. It is hard to say where he properly belonged. Prison seems to be the only place for him that we have. We have a wholesome rational right to demand that our fellow-citizen shall not be "hasty." In this particular case, destiny worked it out. The grave was the best place for him. But not a felon's grave. None of us honestly think suicide a crime. It may sometimes be; but more often it is only the sad conclusion of much preceding sadness. The doctor never called the cowboy a "bad" man.

Two men were playing cards. They had a discussion which appeared (to one of them) to be amicably ended. This one rose to go, the game being finished and the evening late. As he walked away towards the door, the other from behind fired at him. The bullet ploughed a parting in his hair, but it was little more than skin deep. I saw it when it was practically healed. And now comes the significant part of this story. The wounded man asked me, Was there a way to escape being a witness when you had been subpoenaed? His assailant had been duly arrested, and the trial was imminent. My friend had been summoned to testify, and did not wish to. Why? Well, you could never guess; and his reason will be full of freshness to you, unless you know the various workings of the frontier mind better than I did at the time this conversation took place. It seems the wounded man had been carried to bed in a room near by. Next morning, before breakfast, before anything, the other man had come to inquire for him.

"And he blamed himself that thorough, and apologized in such a spirit," said my friend, "that I couldn't feel myself a gentleman if I harbored any feelings."

For a while I suspected him of trifling with my innocence: what game equals the tenderfoot? But he seriously meant what he said, and grieved at learning there was no legal escape from his subpoena. "Damned lawyers," was his final expression.

Now it is not every frontiersman, to be sure, that would pass over with such clemency an attempt to shoot him in the back. Nevertheless, here is an extreme instance of a typical frontier attitude. It was not much to my friend that the man had tried to assassinate him—his hurt was small. The real weight in the scale was that he had chosen to accept the apology. This little affair between gentlemen was settled. What business had the "damned lawyers" to be meddling? Do you perceive how naturally this would be the frontier reasoning?

For what is the frontier but a modern moment of an earlier universal epoch?—the way we all lived before each man had handed over his right of personal vengeance to the law, in exchange for legal protection? What is a policeman but our official deputy whose club relieves us from the necessity of using clubs ourselves? Take away the policeman, and we must all carry clubs again. Now when people left cities and went to live in the Rocky Mountains, they could not pack the policeman with them; and so they had to take a club. You looked out for yourself; there was nobody else to do it for you. And soon, very soon, your primitive nature, that nature which the cradle of convention at best can never do more than lull into a sleep so light as to be scarcely deeper than a doze, waked up with something like a shout of joy. It was so good to take care of your possessions with your own arm and courage! To make a man perform his obligations to you by means of your levelled weapon, instead of by an action for breach of contract! It was so good to carry your life in your hand once more, instead of having it grow stale in the policeman's pocket! So you and your heart and your brain leaped straight from the nineteenth century back to the days of Charlemagne and the Paladins. They used spears, and you a revolver; but this was the only difference. It needed scarce one season to shake you out of your shell of civilization. You lived exercising man's old right of personal vengeance; you had to—or vanish. You lived dealing justice without law; you had to—or vanish. Therefore you lived hand in hand with death, and your eye grew used to death, and your heart fearless of it; so that you held life only a means instead of an end, and you valued other things more, paying your life for them if necessary. And after living so, then to see a fence across the wilderness, to hear of law-suits, to feel civilization creeping westward on your heels was hateful, and savored of the prison.

Hence my friend ran away from the trial to another county. He had been shot; he had forgiven the man; no "damned lawyers" for him!

He embodies the whole frontier. That is the way they felt. I hope it is clear to you that such a code was not only natural and inevitable, but that it did them honor. That New York must have a different code, and that New York must ultimately prevail, does not touch our question. But such a code—and this is the trouble with it—is a strain that human nature cannot stand. It is taking the bridle off and leaving poor human nature to keep the road by itself. The frontier was not really wickeder than you and I and all our acquaintances. Do you doubt this platitude? Then I can only congratulate you upon your unique virtue and your virtuous circle. You don't know anybody who has embezzled? You never heard of a wine or linen merchant labelling things "foreign" that weren't? *Bah!* When I think of some of the people I meet at dinner, I can see them on the frontier, without their bridles. Out there they wouldn't be cheating you in the shop, but at the card-table; they wouldn't be escaping punishment by means of legal machinery, but by killing the sheriff. Possible "bad" men shake hands with you every week. And you yourself—have you never for a few seconds felt like killing somebody? On the frontier you would have done it. Thank your stars for the bridle!

And so at last we reach now our generalizations.

In our three anecdotes we have got at the code of the frontier, the looking after yourself and the light value for human life, and we have met a number of characters. Some of them were hateful, and some not at all so, just as it is in New York. Only their qualities, good and evil, found unbridled expression: that is the difference. Now, how many of these people merely did bad things under pressure, and how many were the genuine article, the "bad" man, the man whose pleasure is to injure you, or whose pleasure involves deliberate injury to you, and whose moral and mental equipment is equal to getting this pleasure successfully? That is the man we are looking for. I find myself hoping you are ready to anticipate and agree with me along the whole line.

Where do you find the bad man? Not in my forgiving friend. But how about the man who shot him in the back? No, not so far as we know him. He came next morning to make what amends he could. An unsafe party to win from at cards; capable of cowardice when enraged; but capable of facing the consequences; a poor shot, not much brains apparently, and with symptoms of decency. He will not do. And certainly the cowboy who tried to kill the doctor will not do. His brain was bad, his heart was good, his nerves unsteady; it is quite likely he never meditated harm in his life; it is probable that, according to his light, he was generous and honest; but life found out his weak spot, and he went under. I have told you about him and the murder he would have done, because the act typifies so many deeds of violence upon the frontier, and exacts the discrimination that must always be made. An Eastern judge said to me quite recently: "There is a vast difference between a criminal act and a criminal disposition." And he went on to say that in his experience of many years, criminal acts were much more common than criminal dispositions. East or West his word is true. He had seen hunger and cold drive decent men and women to theft, sometimes to consequent assault; he had seen old hands inoculate young ones with larceny and burglary, the young hands aware only of the excitement and the compliment of being chosen confederates; he had seen accidental intoxication in a usually sober fellow cause him to do all sorts of mischief. East or West the causes of a criminal act may be legion; and among that legion, cold, deliberate depravity is probably the rarest. I will venture to call the commonest cause excitement—that is, on the frontier. To those men death was often so near, and pistols always so familiar, that environment would breed recklessness in all but the strongest character; thus a visit to town, a game of cards, a horse race, entered upon in the purest friendliness, might end with a burial where nobody was so sorry as the guilty man, and all the rest were sorry for him. Some of the stories, where the case is of a good, fine man whose pistol leaped before it looked, are among the most tragic that I know. I will venture another generalization:

it is not among the chief population of the frontier—namely, the ranchmen, the cow-punchers, the prospectors, and the trappers and huntsmen—that you will usually find the "bad" man. The crimes they commit are almost always of the order that our cowboy would have committed had his arm not been caught in time. The real "bad" man, the perfect specimen, will be among the gamblers, or the stage, bank, and train robbers. Even some of these gentry do it from love of excitement rather than for plunder, just as is the case among Eastern burglars. But if you are predatory, you run a fine chance of growing into a "bad" man, even if you did not start so. And what does it depend on? Why, the qualities of your heart and brain, of course. And now we have our hand on the true "bad" man.

He is in the first anecdote. Not the barkeeper. Not the citizen who could hit cigars so well. He was an unlovely creature, to be sure; and he had one essential piece of the bad man's machinery: his heart was mean enough. We saw that clearly when he failed to respond in the least to the splendid coolness of the boy. The earth was well rid of him. But he was not gifted sufficiently to fill the character; he was too stupid to be dangerous. The boy, however, that rosy, well-clad stripling, meets every demand. He had good manners. He loved peace when not engaged in business. He was mild and clean to see; some "bad" men are not, and their hats and coats and jaws make you suspicious; and then—but truly the boy compels admiration! Think of him once more, with his cigar shot away, instantly devising that diabolic plan and carrying it out. Change his heart, give him kindness, and you would find him high up among Wells Fargo's most valued shot-gun messengers. But you see he had the heart of a demon; and so he practised—we cannot guess precisely his trade, but that he had a trade and was no apprentice at it, we can be sure; whether he dealt cards, or employed dynamite in some connection, matters nothing. He was equal to anything.

One geographic generalization, and we have finished. If you would see the "bad" man to-day, go to the Southwest. It is there he has most flourished, and most survived. There you will find him lower and uglier in depravity than anything I have chosen to tell you. The Northwest has more nearly got him under. The climate and industries there invite more good citizens, and these have their way to a greater extent. The good citizens of Arizona and New Mexico do not have their own way much. Barefaced evil still triumphs there because those deserts favor birds of prey and drive honest men elsewhere. Moreover, Arizona and New Mexico have a special inheritance—the scum from California, Texas, and old Mexico. With this, decency wages a one-sided battle. The tale of train robbery alone in Arizona, and of jury acquittals in recent years when the robbers have been captured, is a black record. One would be neither astonished nor sorry to see vigilantes arise in Arizona and sweep clean the valleys of Sulphur Springs and San Simon.

So here is the end of our quest. We have found some old facts and looked them over anew. Could we hope in reason for more, when it was only human nature we dealt with? We reach the knowledge that the frontier is just ourselves expressed in unbridled terms; that there, as here, average people do bad things and even good people do bad things; that there, as here, the successful fiend is a rarity, because his profession exacts such unusual endowments. For though some are born bad, more achieve badness, or have badness thrust upon them. But we have had a sight of the true "bad" man in the stripling boy with his quiet cigar and his murdering bullet. There he stands in all his symmetry: the clothes of a gentleman, the nerve of a veteran, blooming with adolescence, in cruelty implacable, and perfect in brain. If there is a hell, he will go to it. And so let us take our leave of him.

Theodore Roosevelt: The Sportsman
and the Man

Wister had never been indifferent to political issues, as the preface to Red Men and White *indicated, but by the turn of the century he was readier to articulate a positive vision. This eulogy of Roosevelt as combining the western principles of manliness and the eastern principles of gentlemanliness was clearly a tribute to the recently inaugurated vice-president. Perhaps it was also a way of keeping before the public the name and reputation of a man whom opponents within his own party hoped to bury in that office.*

More important, this essay reveals the extent to which Wister's attitude toward the West had changed. Earlier, it provided spectacle or a test of manhood. In this essay and in "The Open-Air Education," Wister was more interested in what qualities evident in (not caused by) the western environment could be brought east. By redefining the gentleman as manly (and potentially western) rather than effeminate (and European) and by pointing to works rather than to labels, he could present a highly rhetorical defense for the coterie implicitly defined in "The White Goat," place that group at the center of national affairs, and make professional politicians, "albinos," seem less than manly or representative of the real America.

The most extensive account of Wister's relationship with Roosevelt is Roosevelt: The Story of a Friendship 1880–1919 *(New York: Macmillan, 1930).*

Source: Outing 38 *(June 1901): 242–48.*

I T S O H A P P E N S that Mr. Roosevelt was busy fighting the first time that I ever laid eyes on him. This was one afternoon in November, 1878. It also so happens that the last time I saw him he was—yes, fighting is the nearest word to it; for he was defending himself against some thirty-nine voracious, hostile, and incredulous reporters. He was telling them that he did not wish to exchange Governor for Vice-President. It was easy for any one, save apparently the reporters, to see that he meant what he said. The contrast between their faces and his was something for a bystander to remember. His was so entirely genial—precisely as it had been twenty-one years and seven months earlier.

That first occasion was at Harvard College, in the gymnasium, the old round gymnasium by Quincy street and Memorial Hall. The fall athletic meeting had gathered rather more parents, sisters, and admirers, than the building could comfortably hold, to witness the doings of their pet undergraduates. And we obscure freshmen likewise gazed upon the arena from whatever nook in which we had been able to stow ourselves. I pass over the pole jump and the rest of the events, and come at once to Mr. Roosevelt. He was a junior then, and entered for (I think) the middleweight sparring. Anyhow, he stepped in, suitably stripped and suitably covered. His antagonist was a senior, if I remember rightly; and this difference of classes is of itself always enough to season any college contest with an especial spice of rivalry. Mr. Roosevelt had ardent champions in the audience. A particular row of them rises vividly before me at this moment. They dwelt not in Boston but in its neighborhood. I wonder if in present days they ever think of this athletic meeting long ago, and what a herald spark of light it throws upon Mr. Roosevelt's subsequent career? He and the senior sparred for a while, neither one visibly outdoing the other, unless perhaps in coolness; the senior was cooler than Mr. Roosevelt. "Time" was called. Mr. Roosevelt, hearing it, naturally dropped both aggression and defence. But the senior did not at once hear it; and before it had come home to him that the round was over, he had landed a very palpable hit on Mr. Roosevelt's nose, which bled immediately and copiously. At that sight a hiss rose almost fiercely from the onlookers. They knew time had been called. But the hiss could not have lasted two seconds. Mr. Roosevelt turned, or rather whirled round, made a gesture of silence, and in the silence which resulted, said: "It's all right! it's all right! he didn't hear the call." And then, with a smile as amiable and hearty as his voice had been, he shook his antagonist's hand, nodding to him as he did this. A huge roar of clapping went up from the audience; the bloody nose would have been a great card; but a fair game proved a greater one. You may imagine what ardent champions Mr. Roosevelt had during the final round. Nobody cared after that whether the senior showed the more science or not. The judges, if I remember, decided that he did.

All this was near a quarter century ago. As you know him to-day, do you find Mr. Roosevelt changed? Don't you think that Wordsworth's remark about the child being father of the man has here a happy endorsement? To me, as I sit facing this delicate task of speaking publicly about a personal friend, that stormy gust of sympathy in the gymnasium, that roomful of applauding spectators set boiling by the warm contagion of generosity, is merely the prophetic symbol of the present American people, rejoicing to watch in the arena of our politics one figure at least, who, caution or no caution, science or no science, possesses not only the hard shoulder-hitting, but the instant sense of honor of a gentleman. Does any one dislike the word *gentleman* in this connection? Well, that's because he hasn't thought about it any further than the politicians have told him to think. His mental independence has stopped at the line drawn for it by the bosses. Very possibly they have trained him to repeat with a fair imitation of their delicious accent: "The gentleman in politics." That is supposed to dismiss the subject. I have the fortune to think that it doesn't: and we shall return to it presently.

On the 3d of September, 1900, Mr. Roosevelt was in another friendly arena. He and the Democratic candidate for President were invited to speak at the Auditorium in Chicago. You will perceive at once that this in its true nature was precisely as much a "sporting event" as was the match in the Harvard Gymnasium. The Chicago managers of Labor Day entertainments had looked about them for shoulder-hitting talkers, and made their selection with a view to the highest interest attainable. The rules of the game were that the speakers should for this occasion leave campaign politics behind them, should let "Imperialism," and the Philippines, and "Honest Money," and all the rest of it go unmentioned, and talk about something else. Do you remember what happened? The rules of the game were broken again, and Mr. Roosevelt got another bloody nose. "Time" had been called for that day, as it had been called during the old sparring contest. Mr. Roosevelt had heard it, and accordingly dropped aggression and defence, and talked of something else. Here comes the difference. His antagonist, the Democratic candidate, made no mistake about "time;" he knew it had been called. But he went on hitting. He made as crass and wholesale a campaign speech as any of his vocal performances had been. It was a good smart chance to get in some work, you see. Mr. Roosevelt missed this good smart chance. Well, his opponent may have secured by this proceeding some votes; but it estranged a number of people more than anything that he had done so far. I was in the West at the time; and the comment which the West most frequently made about this Auditorium match was, that Mr. Roosevelt had played a "square game." To-day he is Vice-President, and the Democratic candidate is—What is he, exactly?

Now, if you lay these two incidents side by side, the gymnasium event and the Auditorium event, you find the same Mr. Roosevelt in both; he does his fighting on the same old plan; whatever else the years have wrought upon him for better or for worse, he comes out as honorable in Chicago as he did in Cambridge; the game that he plays is "square." And this instinct to be "square," when it goes with a clean, out-of-door sporting and shoulder-hitting nature, wins all hearts at sight, except of course the hearts of politicians. Of them I am not for the moment speaking. They form a class by themselves; a class as distinct from the normal man in its morals as albinos are distinct in their appearance. Of the effect of this special heart-winning quality of Mr. Roosevelt's here is one personal experience as an example. It belongs to a time somewhat before he had become the national figure that he is to-day. It was in November, 1892. The weather was threatening to be cold, and a quantity of snow had already fallen in the valley of the Methow. The tops of the Cascade Mountains had been white for some time. The freight wagon, by which most gradual method of transportation I was seizing a last chance to get out to the railroad from the hunting country where I had lingered, pulled up for some lunch and some rest at a ranch known as "Cheval's." It was away up, deep among the hills to the north of the Columbia river into which the Methow flows. Now Cheval was probably not the owner's name; but he was a Frenchman, somewhat lately come into that country from Medora; and his wife had been, it was said, the maid of the lady whom a certain French marquis, once famous at Medora, had married. Cheval began by being pleasant enough. But when I asked him if he had ever met Mr. Roosevelt near Medora, he became my friend on the spot. Oh, yes, indeed he had known Mr. Roosevelt. How was he? Had I seen him recently? What was he doing? The questions came thick. I told him of the civil service commission in Washington; and he told me that Mr. Roosevelt liked to shoot very much; and that he was "a gentle-man, too, every time." And when our team was again hitched for us to take up our clanking crawl southward through the snow, Cheval was almost fierce because I would not accept his fur coat to keep me warmer when we should be camping at night. No trouble about his getting it back; the freighter would bring it along on his return trip; no matter if that might not be soon.

Do you take in the situation? A freight-team bound away for indefinite days to the railroad across a wilderness where there was little population, and the less said of that the better; and with this freight-team a stranger, a nameless passer-by, whom Cheval would never see again, but who must positively take Cheval's fur coat because he said he knew Mr. Roosevelt! It was not easy to part with my host, leaving the coat behind me. You will pronounce Cheval impulsive. He certainly was. But this enthusiasm cannot be wholly laid to the Gallic temperament. It is, to be sure, the only time that a fur coat has been offered me on the strength of my alleged acquaintance with Mr. Roosevelt; but then it is the single occasion upon which I have seemed to need one. On other western trails, far from the Cascades, when I have happened to pass over ground where Mr. Roosevelt has also been, a mutual acquaintance with him has produced at once a bond between parties who did not previously know each other. His name has always set the company going. The hunters will tell you how he shot something here, or how he missed something there; they will point you out some particularly shelving ledge where they climbed with him, recalling his efforts and his perspiration; they will quote you some remark he made to the cook. And whatever they tell, whether in his favor or at his expense—and they like no mental pleasure so dearly as a tale at your expense—it's all told with a zest and a circumstance that leaves no doubt of their interest in him.

Do not imagine that this is because he is a notability, and that they would recite legends of all notabilities with the same graphic unction. He was not much of a notability in the days that I speak of. They had seen many greater than he. Notabilities are a drug in their market. Their woods have been full of them for long years. Since the Union Pacific's completion, traveling specimens of every European title have been guided by them to some place where they could shoot something, and then have been led safely home from the glorious achievement. Do you remember the Grand Duke Alexis, and his distinguished suite of foreigners, and how one of these was suddenly missing one day? It caused great anxiety to the guides. A guide rode up to the general in command of the expedition, and said: "Please, sir, I'd like to take a look over the ridge. One of them kings has lost hisself." So you see royalty can't surprise them. And they are equally placid over conspicuous Americans. For the city of Washington has emptied senators and secretaries on them. And the New York Central has poured all sorts of magnates over them. They don't mind. They know both dukes and dollars by heart. They welcome the magnificent pay, and forget the people, unless the people are in themselves worth remembering. Mr. Roosevelt was neither dukes nor dollars; but they told me his remark to the cook with profound approbation.

This approbation has followed in his wake from the very first, and he has won it from all classes, save two: those who want him to do better than he can, and those who want him to do worse than he will. The first are citizens of the highest standards. Their expectations of him have been disappointed. They have dropped him. It may be hard to answer the bad things they say, but it is easy to remind them of the good things they omit. Are they quite fair? At all events, their view is colored by no mean motives. The other class are the politicians, the albinos. They have not dropped Mr. Roosevelt. He won't drop; not even when they make him Vice-President. But they would dearly like him to drop, because he is not an albino. He plays "square." He embarrasses them at every turn. They have to swallow him, but if you watch them you'll catch them making a face over the dose. You may catch them, from cabinet ministers down to tobacco-slobbering albinos of the ward. It's an odd experiment to try, and it comes out successful amost always. Talk to the car conductor, or the freight hand, or any such person, and you'll hear him admire Mr. Roosevelt just as the Rocky Mountain guides do. Then find a politician and lead him on. It need not be a Democrat; a Republican does as well. You will find his tone is chilly at once; and pretty soon he'll say something of this sort: "The cowboy business is all very well; but there were plenty of good men in Cuba besides rough riders." There were indeed plenty. Plenty who distinguished themselves, too. Plenty who were better soldiers than Mr. Roosevelt. And there are, perhaps people who write better histories of Cromwell than he does. What then does this prove? That his laurels are unfairly won? Not at all. It proves just what the Rocky Mountains prove; that it is not dukes and dollars, but the man himself which counts with us, and that San Juans and Cromwells have nothing whatever to do with Mr. Roosevelt's success, except in making his character more widely visible to the whole American people.

It is all perfectly clear, and it all comes back to the same thing, the thing we began with in the Harvard gymnasium; the courage, the frank brotherly consideration, and the sense of honor; in one word, the all round gentleman. When you find an all round gentleman who is public spirited and patriotic, you have the very best thing our American soil can produce; and the American people confess this in their approval of Mr. Roosevelt. Do you think the American people don't like a gentleman? Do you suppose that they, whose hearts are full of sport, who admire gameness in every other species, game dogs, game chickens, game horses, stop admiring when it comes to a game man? Would it, in short, be human nature to value the best in every species excepting your own? We are all equal, you say? Man alone of all the animals doesn't belong to the scheme of evolution? Oh no; you know a great deal better than that. You know well enough that those words meant when they were written in the Declaration of Independence. They meant that George Washington and the humblest private in his ranks had equal rights before the law; that they should have equal chances to be as happy as they could. Those words said equal rights to *pursue* happiness, didn't they? The didn't say George Washington and the private *were* equally happy, did they? Any more than they said that they were equally tall, or equally strong, or equally intellectual. But you see you have heard the albinos for years and years declaring that we are all equal; one just as good as the other; that the private could have beaten the British just as well as George Washington beat them. For that's what the albinos' remark amounts to. They go on a little further, about like this: All men are equal. Therefore gentlemen are inferior. That is the albino logic. The truth is, that the albinos are so afraid you will find out that gentlemen—game men, courageous men, generous and considerate and honorable men—are more satisfactory in politics than they themselves are, will govern better, will cost you less and give you more for your money, and will not grow mysteriously rich in office as they do, that they have scared you with a bogey. They have set up for you to laugh at a stuffed figure, labelled "gentleman." This dummy wears strange clothes, walks oddly, speaks oddly, can't fight, has thin legs and no voice, and yellow gloves, and squeaks admiring phrases about England, and weeps over American vulgarity, and is generally too soft to go out in the rain without fear of melting. There are such people, and the albinos tell you that they are "gentlemen." And you have indolently sat and believed this grand lie, and have never used your mind; never asked yourself what George Washington was; never remembered that when you have seen a generous act or a considerate and kind act done by somebody who wasn't obliged to do it and could have been ungenerous and unkind without risk of being found out, that you have exclaimed invariably of such a person: "He's a gentleman!" And so our great people swallow the albinos whole, swallow these moral perverts whom we allow to take charge of our affairs, instead of looking for more people like Mr. Roosevelt. Do you object to the phrase "moral perverts" as applied to politicians? Let me give you a simple illustration that you have often seen. The country needs a certain bill passed. Everybody says it ought to be: everybody knows it ought to be. The party in power which is trying to pass the bill is soon to face a general election. Therefore the party out of power, which hopes to win at that election, defeats the bill in order that the party in power may not get the credit of passing it. No matter about the country. Damn the country. It may be bad for the country, but it's good politics. That's the whole point with the albinos: good politics. And they think that in defeating the bill they have performed their manifest duty. I have taken the simplest instance I can think of; and if that is not moral perversion, pray inform me what is.

Are you inclined to retort on me with this ancient thing: "Ours is a representative government. You cannot expect representatives to be superior to the people they represent." There was a time when I accepted that precious statement, and felt sad to think that the American people resembled their politicians. Then it became my fortune to see something of our people and to hear them often say they would like better representation. To-day this is a very common remark to hear. You see, they are beginning to notice that most politicians never made a dollar in their days until they got an office. And this is so unlike the large majority of our clever and energetic race, that it brings you up with somewhat of a bang against that old thing about our representatives necessarily representing us. If you have accepted that, you have accepted it because it is so universally handed round among us, like ice-cream at a picnic. You take the ice-cream on faith, and now and then it poisons you. Well, the truth is a very different matter. We are mostly busy and responsible; therefore we allow the idle and the irresponsible to get into office under our noses. And the scientific fact about our Republic, as it is now in its great growing ferment, is not that we elect our true representatives, but that in a boiling pot *the scum floats on the surface.* The scum is the albinos, the moral perverts. Contrasted with them Mr. Roosevelt shines, not quite alone, but conspicuous. He takes no mean advantage of an adversary; he stops when "time" is called; he fights "on the square;" he is what the West calls a "white man:" and that is the true cause of him and his great popularity.

The Open-Air Education

By the early years of this century, Wister had become a more frequent commentator on the West than a visitor to it. He was still somewhat confused about the value of the West, or the outdoors in general, since in this essay he states even more overtly than in earlier work that men are born, not made. And his definition of the superior man as the one exhibiting "readiness of brain and promptness of action" has already been embodied in the fictional figure of the Virginian and in the increasingly fictionalized central figure of the Roosevelt cult. But unlike earlier westerners whose wit and readiness Wister had admired, the Virginian had to become a gentleman in order to be a hero—in order, really, to be the true western American.

The trolley accident, in which a Secret Service man was killed and other members of President Roosevelt's party were injured, took place in Pittsfield, Mass., on September 3, 1902 ("President's Landau Struck by Car," [New York Times, September 4, 1902] 1).

The incident of the man who promised Wister "the best horse on the river" was used in "The Gift Horse," where the tenderfoot receives the horse and is nearly lynched because the man he assisted stole it. The story was also published in the Saturday Evening Post 181 July 18, 1908), and in Members of the Family.

Source: Saturday Evening Post 175 (October 25, 1902): 1–2, 22.

DURING THE thirteen months through which the President has been President, can he remember, do you suppose, any day when he would have liked to be merely himself, merely Theodore Roosevelt, for a few moments? Possibly there may be several such days in his recollection, but I shall risk a guess that there has certainly been one. Your mind will doubtless have already told you before I can say what day I mean. It was the time of the late trolley accident; it was when he found himself violently flung from his carriage to the earth, bruised, cut, alive at all only by merciful chance, his companions similarly flung and scattered, while the assaulting cause of all this, the especial curse which the especial blessing of electric cars has brought with it for us all over our country, the typical trolley brute, stood there not sorry and full of desire to be of help, but dense and defiant in his protoplasmic insolence. He was in easy reach of the President's vigorous and expert fists. No one had at first perceived that death as well as bruises had resulted from the lawless outrage. What was visible to every one was the torn and shaken party on the one hand and the trolley brute on the other. If ever a man deserved to be smashed till he could not see out of his eyes, it was now, here in the road, immediately. Physical punishment, wholesome and comprehensible to brutes, would have been far more beneficent than a set investigation by the law, months later, when the world had gone on and the whole affair was cold. Let the company pay damages subsequently, but let the trolley brute pay a black eye now and remember it in running his car hereafter. I am bold enough to reason from what did happen that the President would like to have administered that black eye himself, but alas! where there's a will there's not always a way; many things are forbidden to a President.

You know the details of the incident. Mr. Roosevelt used some good strong English to the man, words as welcome as a tonic breeze on this occasion, welcome to every man and woman in our country, except, of course, those men and women who belong to the neuter gender. Out it came! Shut your ears and scream, ye lady and gentleman neuters, but so did it also come from George

Washington at Monmouth Court House, and so will it come at the proper time from every proper man. But words are a poor make-shift when one has been knocked down in the road, and (remember that I am merely guessing) that moment in September near Mansfield was one when the President would have liked dearly to strip his office from him, as he used to strip his coat in the Harvard gymnasium, and settle his difficulty as a mere man, as he once in Montana settled matters suddenly to the painful surprise of a frontier bully who had taken an imprudent prejudice against Mr. Roosevelt's eyeglasses.

What would Mr. Cleveland have done at Pittsfield? What would Mr. Harrison? or Mr. McKinley? It is useless to surmise, since we can never know; we may be sure that they would have behaved like Presidents. But Mr. Roosevelt behaved like himself. "Don't mind me, I'm not hurt; look after the others," he said, and rushed upon the trolley brute with a few first natural words. And, hearing them, the United States sighed with happy satisfaction. Ah, what a splendid thing is the natural, wholesome man!—the man who thinks straight, feels straight and acts straight; who does not wait to be prompted, but says his say and does his deed outright, and lets criticism begin when he leaves off. We love such a man so much beyond all others that we even want to forgive him when we think he is wrong. He is the man of action, and we prefer him to the man of caution; and not seldom do we find that much caution lies behind his action, caution invisible, caution efficient yet instantaneous, caution that takes in everything and decides in a moment; not that long-drawn-out operation of the mind which keeps people and events waiting. This, indeed, is far better than no caution at all, but it is a poor thing when compared with the quick-working sort. For the quick-working sort not only strikes, *but also knows when to go slow,* and decides upon slowness as quickly as it decides upon everything else.

Can this great gift be won by effort? And if so, where? If it can, I think there is no place so likely as out-of-doors. It is not the body of a man alone that out-of-doors is good for. Have you ever stopped to wonder what George Washington would have been like if he had been brought up in Boston? Mental New England has given us the Emersons and the Hawthornes, but Washington scouted for Indians in the backwoods and Lincoln split rails. So also have the body, the mind and the spirit of Theodore Roosevelt profited by his open-air education. You will remember that he was not a strong boy, that physical health was one of the earliest things that he set his heart upon having, that he sought it in the fields and the woods, following his bent for Natural History, and that he took many rides upon a pony in the same quest. College life did not end this habit, but brought into it certain athletic interests; and, since he became a man, the Rocky Mountains have been a constant recreation—let me spell it *re-creation,* for so you will perceive the word's deep meaning—to Theodore Roosevelt. Whatever his inherited gifts and temperament, be very sure that Nature's schooling has helped him in that directness in deed and word which so often wins and reassures our hearts.

Taught *him,* you may possibly agree, but can it do all these good things for everybody? Please let me say at once that I am not going to preach any panacea to you, not even though I could easily show how much both Emerson and Hawthorne owed to their contact with the open air, and thereby seem to prove that all kinds of men can profit by such education.

No! Since I became acquainted with a certain leering, double-jointed apothegm which states that "No generalization is wholly true—not even this one," I have placed it continually higher in the ranks of wise utterances; and if you will take the twisted thing to heart as I have—sorrowfully—done, you will thenceforth be very wary about your panaceas. You will be careful how you rush about telling your neighbors that anything is the best thing, or the only thing, or the final thing. To believe anything absolutely is very nice, and comfortable, and I do believe that one man's drink may be another man's poison. Open-air education failed so signally with a boy who came under my notice that you must hear the brief incident for the sake of the very useful light that it throws upon panaceas.

He was a farmer's boy, from good rustic stock, brought up in the wholesome fields, and familiar with dogs and horses. He had, to be sure, a vapid, hang-back look to him, but this we, his would-be benefactors, set down to ill health; his lungs were threatened. Therefore we decided that a little cowboy life in the healing air of the West would make a man of him. A friend on a ranch was appealed to and responded most generously; another friend supplied other necessities, and I supplied that copious futility, good advice. The boy went. It was into good hands that he went; good, kind, typical Western hands, ready no doubt to poke fun at him as a tenderfoot, but equally ready to give him a lift through the first steps of his new experience. Well, the whole thing proved a mournful fiasco. The boy began at once to write letters home that sounded like the mewings of a wet cat. He was urged to have patience, but it was no use; the mewings got louder and wetter, and one day the cat came back! Nothing, not the fields of his childhood, nor the horses of his boyhood, nor that inspiring Rocky Mountain splendor of his final experience, had availed. Open-air education could not make a man of this luckless weakling, because there was no man in him to make. I am afraid that men, like poets, must be born so; and fortunately men are more plentiful than poets. We may be sure that nothing ever comes out of a person save that which was originally in him; and you cannot educate a vacuum, not even by the open-air system. Books, travel, open air, all these things are merely fertilizers and if there is no seed in the field no sprouts will appear.

It is not only for the sake of panaceas that I mention the case of the farmer's boy. It is to remind you that a son of the soil can be just as "effete," just as useless a citizen, as those "pampered sons of gold" who are sent to rich colleges by their fathers, the "money barons," and who from time to time are so convenient a mark for the demagogue of the platform or the newspaper when he wants to bring down the gallery. I have seen some effete rich people; but I have seen *rather more* effete poor people. And this is perfectly natural, since riches are apt to be a symptom of force and character, while poverty is often a sign of shiftless weakness. As for college education unfitting young men for practical affairs (you remember that this generalization was announced by a conspicuous Wall Street broker), if you will take the trouble to walk into the offices of the great bankers and brokers of New York and Boston you will find college-bred men sitting high among the seats of success; men of action and caution combined, clear thinkers and hard hitters. Three or four of them stand out prominent as I recall the list known to me, and I find that each rowed on a crew, or played football or baseball. One captain of a winning crew is particularly present to my mind.

There is no call for me to raise my voice in favor of college athletics; it would be inaudible in the already loud chorus; and I would not be among those who by the very extravagance of their praise almost turn us against a good thing. As Mr. Edward Martin says in his recent volume of verse:

> . . . granting a sport is a right good sort,
> Need we make it religion, too?

No indeed! that is where the Too Much comes in, our American failing of exaggeration. My winning crew captain was not a victim of the Too Much. To his training he brought the sobriety gained from much previous open-air education. He was a deep and silent lover of the woods, of the wilderness indeed; and long contact with Nature had brought out both the daring and the restraint of character that was in him. He was able as he matured to astonish the natives of a wild district on one notable occasion. Being desirous to penetrate certain waters with his canoe, he was assured by the inhabitants that such a thing had not been attempted within the memory of man—that the danger from rapids was insurmountable. He listened, and disappeared into the woods. Some weeks afterward he and his companions emerged, having triumphantly accomplished the undertaking. He met at first with entire incredulity, but in the end it was proved to the community; and in those regions today that trip has assumed well-nigh legendary features. Judgment, persistence, independence, these were the qualities developed in the crew captain by his open-air education; and having left a legend behind him in the woods, he sits in a banker's chair passing upon enterprises which involve millions.

Part of his stock-in-trade is shrewd knowledge of men; and this useful gift is one that you will continually meet in those who imbibe learning from the open air. There was a rustic I used to fish with; in the fall he would go shooting, but this I never did with him. It was not money that took him into the open air with his rod and gun, it was not even wholly the desire to catch or to kill something; it was (quite unconsciously to him, I suspect) a passion for out-of-doors, where he observed all the tricks of the wind, and many little habits of little animals. He would expatiate upon the caprices of trout as we do of our male and female acquaintances. You might have supposed he had tried to reason with these fish and show them their absurdities. Now this wandering half savage and wholly delightful creature inquired of me at a time when the neighborhood in general was unanimous in its praise of the new clergyman who had taken charge of one of the two churches, "Seen the parson yet?"

I had not. But he had, with a vengeance.

"Took him fishing." said he to me, "up Turkey Creek. Wouldn't trust him with a nickel."

I could not make him tell me why. I am not certain that he knew himself.

"Oh, well," was all that he would say, "not with a nickel."

Why such destruction of character as this, wrought by simply one day's fishing? It is possible that the man had, under fatigue, or wet feet, or being too cold in the rain, or being too hot in the sun, revealed some flash of his inner self. But if such flash there was, I doubt whether it would have been visible to my less wary observation. I think that the eyes, nay the sum total of sharp senses, that noted the tricks of the wind were alive to signs and symptoms which you and I would not have perceived. At any rate, in not very much more than a year there burst a scandal in that pastoral neighborhood larger than anything that had troubled it for a generation. Ladies hastened about to each other, exclaiming that they refused to believe it, and certainly to the very end some did so refuse. But the clergyman had to go.

You will find this clear reading between the lines of a man's character very common among those whom the open air has educated. It can, of course, be developed as well in other ways, but in none better. And while the open air, with the emergencies it brings, may be doing this service for you, it is likely to be giving you health and promptness at the same time.

A young prospector accidentally shot himself in his tent alone in the mountains. The bullet broke a big hole in the bone of his leg, and he was obliged to remain where he lay, helpless save what his two hands could do for him. It was some hours before his friends returned and found him. It was twenty-four hours before he could be brought to a settlement; and here, after the roughest sort of journey down the mountains, there was no doctor. There was nothing but listerine and frontier intelligence, the quick, sure intelligence bred of constant emergencies. Bandages were made while the doctor was waited for, and he had to be summoned from seventy-five miles away by a messenger on horseback. It was the third day (I almost think it was the fourth, but I will be sure of no overstatement) following the accident when the doctor reached his patient, and we had all made up our minds sorrowfully and silently that the poor fellow must lose his leg up to the knee, that this forfeit was the lightest with which he could get off. After inspecting the wound, which was a horrible-looking thing, I assure you, the doctor declared that he could do nothing safely so far from proper appliances and proper nursing, and that the patient must be taken to the hospital at the nearest town. This happened to be Spokane, and it meant a three days' journey for the wounded man—two of them in a stage. He fought against the doctor as one fighting for his life. He piteously asseverated that he would recover there, that once in the hospital they would take off his leg to a certainty that he knew he could get well and keep his leg if only he were allowed to stay there. To every argument he had but these words to repeat, and they prevailed. That is, he was allowed to take the risk at his own peril, and the doctor departed, back seventy-five miles to where he lived. The directions that he left about bandaging and washing were devotedly and efficiently carried out, not by a woman, but by a man; a man college-bred, to which education had been added a most strenuous schooling of the open air. Once the doctor visited his patient again, and that was all. There was no fever, no illness, nothing but a steady healing of bone and flesh. I saw it every day with my own eyes, and I have seen nothing more marvelous ever. Some four weeks later I went to bid the man good-by. I found him at a ranch among the hills, hopping about on crutches for caution's sake, and blithe as a bird. He and his leg still keep company.

The same rich physical and moral gifts of health and promptness bred by the open air brought a young fellow through an accident in a corral scarcely less serious. A wild horse that he was trying to rope plunged and fell, crushing the bones of his ankle shapeless. They carried him into a cabin, where there was nothing but some laudanum of mine to help his sufferings. This time the hospital was only seventy-five miles away, and everybody volunteered to take him there, or make him comfortable on the long, rough drive. It was late in October, at an altitude of some seven thousand feet. One brought quilts, another blankets, a third furnished the easiest-running wagon within reach, a fourth horses, and two drove him away after nightfall down the river. I sent a note to the doctor, whom I knew; but the note effected nothing, for the attention the boy received was the same admirable care shown to every one. Three or four weeks later he, too, was out of hospital and hopping about on crutches. He thought, quite unnecessarily, that he owed some thanks to me. These he did not, of course, directly express. Open-air education makes such expressions extremely difficult. But I suspected by the way in which he lurked about that he was troubled, so to speak, with subcutaneous thanks; and I therefore casually mentioned my regret that the note I had sent the doctor had done no good, that the treatment he received was the same anybody would receive, and that I had been in no way allowed to make myself responsible. These remarks brought none from him, neither did they change his mind about thanks. As I was stepping into the stage to leave the country for that season he was on hand. He did not say "Good by"; that seems to be a rare and objectionable word in the open air. He said, looking away from me in a guilty manner, "Next year you'll have the best horse on the river."

We began our instances with a trolley car, and I am going to let the last one be connected with the same vehicle; for you will see, I think, that it assembles and presents all the benefits that can be got from open-air education. This time it is the back instead of the front of the car that is involved, and thus we get all the ugly characteristics of the street car—characteristics that ourselves are alone to blame for. You know that Herbert Spencer has said we Americans are losing our love of liberty. I hope that he is wrong, but I know very well what he means. We suffer a host of daily routine impositions rather than do what is called "make a kick." We suffer these things not at all from good nature, but from a species of cowardice; and to cover this cowardice up and preserve our self-esteem we have invented the word "kicker." "Thank heaven," a man exclaims, "I am not a kicker." And then he goes and pays an unjust bill rather than dispute it. And if you ask, Why? he will be apt to say. "Oh, let us live and let live!" After that he feels comfortable because he has got round the corner from his cowardice. But it is there just the same. If he had disputed his bill the next man would do it, too, and presently bills would be correct. If everybody treated the motorman as the President did, presently motormen would be more careful. And as for the trolley-car conductor—here we come to the rear end of the machine and find standing on it all too frequently a special sort of coward, the sort who refuses to turn a drunken and disorderly passenger out of the car, and mutters by way of defense, "He's paid his fare, and he's got as good a right to ride as anybody."

You have probably met this specimen yourself. He, like the motorman, usually knows that a powerful corporation, if not a political pull, stands behind him, and that your sufferings and complaints, unless you happen to be President of the United States, will not weigh much with his employees. Thus are you and I, the public, ground between the upper and nether millstone of capital and labor because we are afraid to be "kickers." One afternoon a case of this grinding was taking place in Philadelphia. The car was bound uptown, and business men and shopping women filled it fairly well. Among them sat a citizen, quite dirty and quite drunk. He was an offense to decency, a public nuisance; he had no business to be there. The conductor knew this, and therefore took good care not to see the citizen. The citizen (as is frequent) had a cigar, not in his mouth but in his hand, and the fumes of it rose and stank in the car. Of course smoking was expressly forbidden; but you know this trick of the cigar in the hand. You know also what we men were all doing. We were behind our papers, or otherwise pretending that nothing was the matter, or else making a smile and a wink of it to fool our consciences. I take it we were few of us secretly at ease, because the cigar and the drunkenness of the man was plainly annoying to two women. They, poor things, dared to make no more complaint than we did, and for the same reason, they were afraid to be conspicuous; they shrank from a scene they chose rather to suffer an ill-smelling invader of their rights than be stared at for telling the conductor to do his duty.

Thus we should have all continued to journey in among Philadelphia tolerance of the intolerable but for a refreshing interruption. There sat among us in the plain clothes of labor one who was not of ourselves. Living in Philadelphia had not yet cured him of his independence. He had earned his bread west of the Missouri, sometimes as a cowboy and sometimes as a soldier, and he now proceeded to disclose all the symptoms of his training.

"Conductor," said he with a pleasant intonation (and we all came from behind our papers), "that man ought to have been put out some time ago."

The conductor went through quite a performance of being busy with his exchange tickets.

"You heard me, conductor," said the passenger (I wish I could make you hear his pleasant intonation), "but it's not too late yet."

At this the drunken man began to show some symptoms too. He looked bovine and belligerent, while the conductor was now forced to play his customary false ace of trumps.

"He's paid his fare. He's got as good a right to ride as you have."
But the passenger played his joker.

"You'd not say that if he had smallpox. Well, I'll have to get out
myself." And he walked out of the door.

"Who says I got smallpox?" roared the drunken man, furiously
following the passenger to the platform, where he was seized up
by the quick muscle of the West and set down in the track behind,
and the car went on without him.

Here is open-air education for you, and applied just right! This
man who had got his full growth made the rest of us men in that
car look small. He stood head and shoulders above us in a number
of ways, among which muscular strength was the least important.
Indeed, it may well be that in the mere matter of throwing a man
off a car there were others present as able as he. But brute force is
not the point, for this can easily be developed in a gymnasium.
Nor even is readiness of brain or promptness of action quite the
point, though both are marks of the superior man. It was unques-
tionably superior (so at least I think) to play that drunken citizen
like a trout and land him; to observe decorum first by an appeal to
the conductor, then, after sizing up the victim, to mention smallpox and thereby instantly accomplish a whole rapid design. No
tussle in the car, no fright for the ladies, the entire business
dispatched neatly on the back platform! I envied him very much
such brains and quickness, such perfect coordination between
thought and act; I envy him to-day. But the still more precious
thing which he possessed, and which I do not, was his unconscious and absolute independence. He had a mind, he made it up,
he went ahead. He did not stop to look right and left at the
bystanders. Let them stare if they want to! He cared not a baubee
or picayune.

That man of the people who had got his full of growth by open-air
education, who put us smoothly dressed and smoothly conducted
civilians to shame, who respected the women, snubbed the conductor, and abated a nuisance, all as easy as rolling off a log,
would have pleased Herbert Spencer as much as he pleased me.
And into my head he has put this exclamation:

Oh, the blackmail that we pay to convention! the petty, cowardly tons of blackmail! We must not live east of a certain street because "nobody does." We must spend our summers in certain places because "everybody does." For the sake of nobody and everybody we squander dollars upon things that we do not want and abstain from other things that we very much want. The bystanders are always with us; whenever we take an unusual step we peep and squint to see how the bystanders are looking. In fact, it is chiefly through the eyes of the bystanders, and not our own, that we look at life. Thus may a man dialogue with his soul. "I question Universal Suffrage." "Better not. The crowd will hoot you." "I should like to be a Baptist." "Better not. Society is Episcopalian." "I intend to have tea instead of late dinner in summer." "You can't. Newport dines at eight-thirty." And so on from the sublime down the whole ladder; but it is all ridiculous.

Let nobody suppose that I suppose convention is an unmitigated evil. We all of us know that it is an imperative necessity; but I do not purpose to let it bleed me of my principles, my pleasures or my purse, or in any way whatever rub me out. I have seen too many people rubbed out by it.

How, then to get rid of the bystanders? How to see things as they are and not as somebody else sees them? For the average man I recommend as much open-air education as his walk in life makes possible for him. I am claiming no panacea here, pray remember. I don't promise that thus you will become either George Washington or Emerson. But if you have noted the more humble graduates of the open air that I have here enumerated you will find that all of them show the same signs of health and independence commensurate with their several abilities; they do not get entangled in other people's opinions. And I think (unless you are like the farmer's boy) that if you frequent nature and the primitive life you will be likely to attain your full growth and grow entirely out of the reach of convention the blackmailer.

The Mountain Sheep: His Ways

The difference between this essay and "The White Goat" is not just a matter of reminiscence vs. observation or reporting vs. self-quotation but a matter of style and voice. While the early Wister wrote in several voices, he was unconscious of doing so. Here, the successful author looks back on the period when he was "still too much one of the guided" and condescends both to that earlier self and to his guides. He is much more likely to use analogy and to compare animal and human behavior in matters of sentiment and class, and he is far more likely to moralize. The author of this piece is, if more confident and efficient, much less open to experience than his younger self had been.

The observation about the sheep tethered in Livingston, Montana, was the only thing Wister ever published about his mysterious trip from Philadelphia to Cinnibar, Wyoming, July 2–14, 1892. The ostensible reason was to tell George West, his guide, that he could not go hunting with him. Darwin Payne and others have speculated that Wister did not want to stay in Wyoming because of the aftermath of the Johnson County War—his friends were on the losing side, and resentment had not died down. On the other hand, he did not want to seem afraid to come at all.

Wister obviously consulted diaries when writing the essay. The drive in 1885 during which he saw a number of sheep took place on July 21 and is recorded in Owen Wister Out West *(36–37). Wister had noted his intention to write "The Adventures of a Bad Shot" in 1891 (125) rather than 1888. His companions on the mismanaged sheep hunt of August 30, 1888, were Bobby Simes and the guides Dick Washakie and Paul LeRose. The diary focuses on the hunters' reactions, not on the sheep (80–85), but the sequence of events and many of the phrases are taken directly from the diary. However, Wister cuts from the published account Simes's part in the hunt and describes the pillared rocks as looking like sinister altars rather than the diary's version, in which they look "as if large children had built them for diversion."*

No account of the 1896 trip is preserved in Owen Wister Out West.

Source: Musk-Ox, Bison, Sheep and Goat, *edited by George Bird Grinnell and Caspar Whitney (New York: Macmillan Company for the American Sportsman's Library, 1904), 171–222, including illustrations. Scientific descriptions and speculations have been omitted in the version here reprinted.*

U PON A Sunday morning, the 10th of July 1892, I awaked among my scanty yet entangling Pullman blankets, and persuaded the broken-springed window-shade of my lower berth to slide upward sufficiently for a view of Livingston, Montana. Outside I beheld with something more than pleasure a fat and flourishing mountain ram. He was tethered to a telegraph pole, and he scanned with an indifference bred by much familiarity our sleeping-car, which had come from St. Paul, being dropped last night from the coast-bound train, because it was this morning to trundle its load of tourists up the Yellowstone Park branch to Cinnabar. The ram had been looking at Eastern tourists and their cars long enough for the slow gaze of his eye to express not a kindred but the same contempt which smouldered in the stare of the Indians at Custer station, of the cow punchers at Billings, of every Rocky Mountain creature, indeed, beneath whose observation the Eastern tourist passes. Dear reader, go stand opposite the lion at the zoo if you don't know what I mean. So patent was the stigma cast that it fantastically came into my head to step down and explain to the animal that I was not a tourist, that I had hunted and slain members of his species before now, and should probably do so again. And while thus I sat speculating among the Pullman blankets, the ram leaped irrelevantly off the earth, waved his fore legs, came down, ran a tilt at the telegraph pole as though at a quintain, and the next instant was grazing serene on the flat with an air of having had no connection whatever with the late disturbance.

What had started him off like that? Extreme youth? No; for when I came to hear about him, he was five years old—a maturity corresponding in us men to about thirty. It was simply his own charming temperament. No locomotive had approached; moreover for locomotives he, as I was later to observe, did not care a hang; no citizen old or young of either sex had given him offence; nor was there stir of any kind in Livingston, Montana, this fine early Sunday morning. When I presently stood on the platform, only the wind was blowing down from the sunny snow-fields, and that not bleakly, while from high invisible directions came thinly a pleasant tankling of cow-bells.

Not two minutes had I been on the platform when the ram did it again. Yes, it was merely his charming temperament; and often since, very often, when encompassed with ponderous acquaintance, have I envied him his blithe and relaxing privilege. I was now thankful to learn that the branch train had still some considerable time to wait for the train from Tacoma, before it could take me from the ram's company; no such good chance to watch a live healthy mountain sheep on his own native heath was likely again to be mine, and after breakfast I sought his owner at once.

"It's a fine dy," said the owner.

"And a very fine ram," I assured him.

"He's quite tyme," the owner went on. "You can have him for five hundred."

"You're a long way from London," was my comment; and he asked if I, too, were English. But I was not, nor had I any wish to bear away the ram, skipping and leaping into civilization.

Three hundred pounds would, I suppose, have been a little heavier than he was, but not much; he stood near as high as my waist, and he had at some period of his long, long ancestry marched across to us from Asia upon his lengthy un-sheeplike legs—skipped over the icy straits before Adam (let alone Behring) was in the world, and while the straits themselves waited for the splitting sea to break the bridge of land between Kamchatka and Alaska. This is the best guess which science can make concerning our sheep's mysterious origin. Upon our soil, none of nature's graveyards hold his bones preserved until late in the geological day; earlier than the glacial period neither he nor his equally anomalous comrade, the white goat, would seem to have been with us; and we may comfortably suppose that sheep and goat took up their journey together and came over the great old Aleutian bridge which Behring found later in fragments. Having landed up there in the well-nigh Polar north, they skipped their way east and south among our Pacific and Rocky Mountains, until, by the time we ourselves came over to live in the North American continent, they had—the sheep especially—spread themselves widely, and were occupying a handsome domain when we met them.

"Among other things we procured two horns of the animal . . . known to the Mandans by the name of ahsahta . . . winding like those of a ram."

This, so far as I know, is the first word of the mountain sheep recorded by an American. Thus wrote Lewis on December the twenty-second, 1804, being then in winter camp with the Mandan Indians, not many miles up the river from where to-day the Northern Pacific's bridge joins Bismarck to Mandan. We find him again, on the twenty-fifth of the May following, when he has proceeded up the Missouri a little beyond the Musselshell, writing, "In the course of the day we also saw several herds of the big-horned animals among the steep cliffs on the north, and killed several of them;" as to which one of his fellow explorers correctly comments in his own record, "But they very little resemble sheep, except in the head, horns, and feet." It is not worth while to quote a later reference made when the party was near the Dearborn River, north, sixty miles or so, of where now stands the town of Helena.

Thus it is to be seen that Meriwether Lewis, private secretary to President Jefferson and commander of that great expedition, met the mountain sheep in Dakota and from there to the Rocky

Mountains grew familiar with him; though not so familiar as to prevent his later making a confusion between sheep and goats, which, being handed down, delayed for many years a clear knowledge of these animals. To this I shall return when goats are in question.

Until very lately, until the eighties, that is to say, sheep were still to be found in plenty where Meriwether Lewis found them among the Bad Lands of Dakota; and they dwelt in most ranges of the Western mountains from Alaska to Sonora. They had not taken to the peaks exclusively then; the great table-land was high enough for them. I very well recall a drive in July, 1885, when, from the wagon in which I sat, I saw a little band of them watching us pass, in a country of sage-brush and buttes so insignificant as not to figure as hills upon the map. That was between Medicine Bow and the Platte River. To meet the bighorn there to-day would be a very extraordinary circumstance; and as for Dakota, there too has civilization arrived; and you will find divorces commoner than sheep—and less valuable.

It is Gass whom I have cited above as to the scant likeness between this wild so-called sheep and the usual sheep of our experience; and it was Gass whose word I remembered this Sunday morning at Livingston, while I stood taking my fill of observation. The ram, as his owner had assured me, was in all truth quite "tyme"; and you could examine him as near as you wished. I took hold of his rope and pulled him to me, and rubbed his nose. Like a sheep? I have already spoken of this long legs. I now looked him over carefully for a sign of anything in the nature of fleece. There was no sign. Short hair, in texture not unlike the antelope's and in color not far from that gray we see in fishing-line, covered him close and thick. Upon his neck and shoulders it merged with a very light reddish brown, and on his rump it became a patch much lighter, though not white. In fact, the hue of his coat varied subtly all over him; and I am tempted to remark in this connection that in describing the color of wild animals most of us have been apt to make our assertions far too rigid. Animals there are, of course, completely white, or black, and so forth; but many, the more you scrutinize them, the more reveal gradations, as this ram did; gray fishing-tackle is only a rough impression of his tint upon the 10th of July; on December the 1st of that same year I saw him again, and his hair had darkened to something like a Maltese cat's. Furthermore, I have seen other sheep in summer that struck me, some as lighter, and some as darker, than the gray of fishing-tackle. And what, shall we infer, do these variations import? Adjustments to climate and environment, state of the individual's age and health, or several distinct species of sheep? I think I should be shy of the last inference unless I were prepared to accept a difference in the color of the eyes and hair of two brothers as being a basis sufficient to class them as separate subspecies of man. . . . So now at length, you who have never looked upon him, see him, if you can, through my unscientific vision, as I rubbed his nose at Livingston, Montana: tall almost as a deer, shaped almost like a heavy black-tail deer, close haired, grayish, tailless, with unexpected ram's horns curving round his furry ears and forward, with eyes dark yellow and grave, and with the look of a great gentleman in every line of him. The tame sheep is hopelessly *bourgeois;* but this mountain aristocrat, this frequenter of clean snow and steep rocks and silence, has, even beyond the bull elk, that same secure, unconscious air of being not only well bred, but *high* bred, not only game but *fine* game, which we still in the twentieth century meet sometimes among men and women. What gives distinction? Who can say? It is to be found among chickens and fish. What preserves it we know; and our laws will in the end extirpate it. Many people already fail to recognize it, either in life or in books. But nature scorns universal suffrage; and when our houses have ceased to contain gentlefolk, we shall still be able to find them in the zoölogical gardens.

During my interview with the sheep, freight trains had passed once or twice without disturbing him or attracting his notice; but as I walked away and left him grazing, there came by a switching-engine that made a great noise. This didn't frighten him, but set him in a rage. Once again he leaped into the air waving his fore legs and eccentrically descended to charge with fury his telegraph pole. Yes, he was "tyme," if by that word one is to understand that he was shy neither of men nor locomotives; but just here there is a hole in our dictionary. Do you imagine that five years of captivity are going to tame the blood and the nerves of a creature that came over the Aleutian bridge from Asia during the Pleistocene, and has been running wild in the mountains until 1887? He was "tame" enough to pay you no attention—until he wanted to kill you; and this was what he did want when I saw him on the first day of the following December. Then was his rutting time; he was ready to attack and destroy with his powerful horns anything in Livingston; and so it was in a stable that I found the poor fellow, took a peep through the quarter-opened door, where his owner had shut him and tied him in the dark, away from his natural rights of love and war. I noted his winter coat of maltese, I heard his ominous breathing, I saw the wild dangerous lustre in his rolling eye; and that was my farewell to the captive.

So good a chance to study a live ram I have never had again. Upon the other occasions when I have been able to approach them at all, study has not been my object, and the distance between us has been greater; but on one happy later day, I watched a ewe with her lamb for the good part of a morning.

In the summer of 1885, as I have said, the mountain sheep had not yet forsaken quite accessible regions in Wyoming; and very likely he still came down low in most of his old haunts. The small band which I saw was not many miles from one of the largest ranches in that country, and the creatures stood in full sight of a travelled road,—not at that time a stage-road, but one that might be daily frequented by people riding or people driving on their way north from Medicine Bow into the immense cattle country of the Platte and of the Powder River still farther beyond, all the way to the Bighorn Mountains. Those very mountains that bear the sheep's name and were once so full of sheep as well as of every other Rocky Mountain big game are now sacked and empty. Hidden here and there, some may exist yet, but as fugitives in a sanctuary, not as free denizens of the wild. I saw three years bring this change which thirty years had not brought; and in 1888 you would have looked in vain, I think, for sheep on the road from Medicine Bow to Fetterman. I found them that year at no such stone's throw from the easy levels of the earth, but up in the air a great distance.

The Washakie Needle, for steepness, is truly a heartrending

country, and that is why the sheep are there. In it rise Owl Creek, Grey Bull, and certain other waters tributary to the Bighorn; and I have never gone with pack-horses in a worse place. A worse place, in fact, I have never seen; though they tell me that where Green River heads on the Continental Divide (in plain sight from the Washakie Needle across the intervening Wind River country) you can, if you so desire, enmesh yourself, lose yourself among cleavages and cañons that slice and slit the mountains to a shredded labyrinth. From the edge of that rocky web I stepped back, discouraged, a year later; and for vertical effects the Washakie Needle remains, as they say, "good enough" for me. We struggled to it through a land of jumping-off places, a high, bald, bristling clot of mountains that, just beyond the southeast corner of the Yellowstone Park, come from several directions to meet and tie themselves into this rich tangle of peaks, ledges, and descents. You really never did see such a place! and my memory of it is made lurid by an adventure with a thunder-storm which cannot be chronicled here* because it happened on one of the days when we found elk, but most lamentably missed our sheep. Missing a sheep, let me say, is of all missing the most thorough that I know.

Encouragement, false encouragement, had come to us after our very first night in camp by the Washakie Needle. The next night we had wild mutton for supper. That initial day, Wednesday, August twenty-ninth, brought us this sweet luck, sweet not alone in its promise of more (for the country was evidently full of sheep), but almost equally because of late, during our perilous journey, we had come down to bacon. Now, to be a hunting party, to be in the Shoshone Mountains in August, 1888, and to be eating *bacon,* was to be humiliated; only our hard travelling that allowed no attending to other business could excuse such a bill of fare; hence did our pride and our stomachs hail this wild mutton. There was not much of him to hail: he was a young ram; and between six of us, after bacon . . . need I say more?. . . .

Four of us were so foolish as to set out together upon this evil

*See "An Electric Storm on Washakie Needle," *Science* 28 (December 11, 1908): 837–39.

morning; two parties, that is, of the guide and the guided. There is never any gain in doing this, and almost always loss. The attention which you should be giving to your business is divided by conversation, or by waiting for some member of the party who has fallen behind; and no matter how silent you keep your-selves, four people are sure at some wrong moment to prove conspicuous; better hunt alone, unless circumstances make it wise that there should be two of you—steep country does make this wise—but assuredly never go after game in fours, as we two white men and two Indians went now. We labored and we la-bored and we finally were upon the top instead of at the bottom of something. It was no more than a ridge, not high, that every-where dropped off into our own valley or the next one; but two sweating hours had gone in getting merely here, and here our eight eyes discerned sheep, quite a band of them. Not, however, before the sheep had discerned us four wily hunters. We did not know this then, because they stayed still where they seemed to be grazing. It was a great way off in a straight line through the air, for the sheep were small dots upon the mountain; and there was no straight line for us to reach them by. We labored and we labored down to a new bottom and upward on a new slope, and made a most elaborate "sneak," crouching, and stopping, and generally maneuvering among stones, gravel, and harsh tufts of growth; so did we come with splendid caution upon where the sheep had been, and, lifting our heads, beheld the vacuum that they had left, and themselves contemplating us from the extreme top of the mountain. I am sure that you know how it feels to have your foot step into space at what you thought was the bottom of the staircase. There is a gasp of very particular sensa-tion connected with this, and that is what I had now, followed at once by the no less distasteful retrospect of myself with my half-cocked rifle, crawling carefully for yards upon my belly, while the sheep watched me doing it. There they were on the top of this new mountain, away far above us, and we four hunters pro-ceeded to go on wrong, as we had begun. I have forgotten to mention that, among our other follies, we had brought horses. Never do such a thing! If you are not in training good enough to hunt mountain sheep on your own legs, wait and climb about for a few days until you have got your breath. What my horse did for me on this precious day was this: our hills were too steep for him to carry me up, so I led him; they were too steep for him to carry me down, so I led him; and betweenwhiles, when I was stalking sheep, I naturally had to leave him behind, and naturally had to go back for him when the stalk was over. You will have by this time but a middling opinion of my common sense; but please bear in mind that Shoshone Indians invariably hunt with horses, and that in those days I was still to much one of the "guided" to be equal to dictating to any Indian what trail we should go, and in what manner we should hunt. This entire hunt of 1888, from the distant Tetons and the waters of Snake River over to the Washakie Needle and Owl Creek, is a tale of struggle between ourselves and our red-skinned guides; we were beginning to know the mountains, to crave exploration, to try the unbeaten path; and for an Indian (though you would never suspect it until you suffered from it) the *un*beaten path is the one that he never wishes to try and will do all things to escape—even to deserting you and going home.

We hunters now set our legs to new laboring, and presently were again weltering in sweat, and could look down into a third valley similar to the two we had so painfully quitted. Down at the bottom of this new gash in the hills went a little stream like all the others, and beyond bristled interminably the knife-like intersections of the mountains. We had placed our sheep behind a little rise along the summit, and between this and ourselves some three hundred yards still intervened. We were, of course, much above where any trees grew, and the ground was of that stony sort with short growth and no great rocks immediately near; a high, lumpy pasture of mounds and hollows, wet with snows but lately melted, hailed upon often, rained on but seldom. Lower down, this pasture country (which made the top of all but the highest and severest mountains) fell away in descents of gravel and sheer plunges of rock. To get closer to our sheep we now discovered we must go down some of this hill we had just come up; they were on the watch, but were fortunately watching the wrong place, and we

all sat down in happy pride for a consultation. The other side of
the hill had turned out suddenly to be a precipice, a regular
jumping-off one, that went a long way and ended in a crumble of
shifting stones, and then took a jump or two more and so reached
the water at the distant bottom. This side was our only possible
course, and we took another look at the sheep. They had given up
watching, and in joy we started for them quickly. We had so
skilfully chosen the ground for our approach that we were
screened by a succession of little rises and hollows which lay
between us and the sheep. This time, this time, there was to be no
crawling up to find a vacuum, no raising your head to discover the
departed sheep taking a bird's-eye view of you! What the hearts of
the other hunters did, I don't know, but my heart thumped with
vindictive elation as we sped crouching among the little intervening hollows, perfectly hidden from the sheep and drawing close to
them at last. Only one more rise and hollow lay between us and
where they were pasturing; and over that rise we hastened straight
into the laps of some twenty sheep we had known nothing about;
they were all lying down. Neither had they known anything about
us; the surprise was mutual. All round me I saw them rise, as it
were, like one man and take to diving over the precipice. Bewilder-
ment closed over me like a flood; all my senses melted into one
blurred pie of perception in which I was aware only of hind legs
and hopping. Frightful language was pouring from me, but I
didn't hear what it was; all was a swirl and scatter of men and
sheep. Not one of us hunters was ready with his gun or his
intelligence. We indiscriminately stampeded to the edge, and there
went the sheep, hustling down over the stones, sliding, springing,
and dissolving away. And now, suddenly, when it was of no use at
all, we remembered that we carried rifles, and like a chorus in a
comic opera we stood on the brow of the mountain, concertedly
working the levers, firing our Winchesters into space.

  It's all fifteen years ago; yet as I read over my relentless camp-
diary, I blush in spite of laughter; it's hot work staring truth in the
face! And now comes the last feeble pop of the ridiculous. We
turned our heads, and beheld the sheep we had come for, the sheep
we had climbed two mountains for, the sheep we had at length got

within an hundred yards of, just disappearing over a final ridge so far away that there remained to them no color, and only one dimension—length. They looked like a handful of toothpicks. They naturally had not been idle while we were so busy; while we were losing our heads, they had kept theirs; and during that brief fusillade of ours—the whole preposterous affair could not have filled more than three minutes—they had put such a stretch of ups and downs between us, that going after them any more was not to be thought of.

We stood at the empty top of the mountain with our ruined day. There was not a live animal in sight anywhere. Those that jumped into the valley were lost among the pines, and warned about us beyond retrieve. We had banged away at such a rate up here that a wide circle of sheep must be apprised of our neighborhood. Why had we done it? For just the same reason that a number of brave persons ran away suddenly at Bull Run as if perdition were at their heels. Surprise, I take it, is at the bottom of the most unaccountable acts of men. And if you wonder why our two Indians were surprised, I can only answer with a theory of mine that Indians who hunt on horseback have small knowledge of mountain sheep. Antelope, deer, white-tail and black, and even elk, can be, and are constantly thus hunted by the Indians; but when it comes to climbing where the horses cannot go, I suspect that his rider seldom goes either. Looking back, I see now that this whole excursion was conducted ignorantly, and that our guides (both of them excellent hunters of other game) neglected the very first principle here, namely, to get to the top of the mountains and hunt down.

We returned our long way to camp, and the elk that one of us shot at sundown made no atonement for our melancholy farce. My diary concludes, "So ended Thursday, August 30, a most instructive day, full of weather, wind, and experience."

By breakfast we were bearing up a little, making much of the fact that, after all, the sheep we had seen were only ewes and lambs. This would not have caused us to spare them, to be sure; we were out of fresh meat when we saw them; and though the head and horns of a ewe do not make a noble trophy for the sportsman, they represent hard work, and are decidedly better than nothing at all when you are a beginner, and hungry.

We took another course, making for mountains on the side of the valley opposite from yesterday's route. My Indian was not hopeful. "Too much shoot," he remarked. "Run away." But presently we passed very fresh tracks, and began one of those ascents where you are continually sure that the next top is the real top. We had come looking for the sheep at a season when he is living mostly upon the roof of his house. He, with the goat, inhabits, it may be fairly said, the tallest mansion of all our ruminants; indeed, you may put the whole case thus:—

Our Rocky Mountains are a four-story building. The bottom is the sage-brush and cottonwood, the second is pines and quaking-asp, the third is willow bushes, wet meadows, and moraines, and the fourth is bald rocks and snowfields. The house begins about five thousand feet high, and runs to fourteen thousand. We have nothing to do with the prairie-dog and others that live in the cellar; it is the antelope to which the first floor belongs, and also the white-tail deer, which, however, gets up a little into the second. The elk, the black-tail, and the muledeer possess second and third stories in common, while the fourth is the exclusive territory of the sheep and the goat. But here is the difference; these latter (the sheep, certainly) descend to all the other stories if the season drives or the humor suits them; they go from roof to ground, while the other animals seldom, save when hunted, are to be met above or below their assigned levels. I have met a sheep on Wind River in July where the sage-brush was growing, and another on a wooded foot-hill just above Jackson's Lake.

This day we went to the fourth story by a staircase dear to the heart of a sheep. I mounted through an uncanny domain where all about me stood little pillars of round stones baked together in mud, and planted on end, each supporting a single rock of another color set upon them transversely; shafts of necromancy they would have seemed in the age of witches, altars which might flame by night while some kind of small, naked beings with teeth held rites over the traveller's crushed body, for from one's feet here the little stones rolled down to right and left into depths invisible. You who have not seen cannot imagine how here and there in the Rocky Mountains these masonries of nature suggest the work not of men but demons. Silence drew around me as I passed upward through the weird dwarf Stonehenge; and on top we found ourselves looking down the other side at a gray stump which presently moved. The glasses showed us the stump's legs and fine curling horns; and our hearts, which had been for some time heavy at the poor luck, grew light. Only, how to get at him?

We had almost given up the game when we spied the ram; we had come so far for so long; and we now had been sitting upon—almost straddling—this ultimate ridge, with the Indian every little while lugubriously repeating, "No sheep." The ram had not a suspicion of us, and presently lay down in the sun near the bottom of a rocky gulch. The whole of the gulch we could not see, not even when we had crawled down a side of the mountain, an endless surface of rolling stones with scanty patches of grass and an occasional steadfast rock. This descent seemed the most taxing effort yet. It was nearly always (and sometimes quite) impossible to stir a foot or a hand, or shift any fraction of my weight, without starting a rippling stream of stones that chuckled and bounced and gathered noise as they flowed downward, and finally sprang into a rocky chasm which gave out hollow roars. I often felt certain these sounds must reach the ram; but they were only next door to him, so to speak, and separated by the tilted wall of mountain which divided his gulch from the one down the side of which I was so very gradually making my way. I don't believe the whole distance could have been more than three hundred yards; yet I was nearly thirty minutes accomplishing it with the help of the grass tufts and every other fixture that came within available reach in this sliding sea of stones. I at length arrived where I wanted to be, and a truly unkind thing happened: I was taken with "buck fever"! It didn't prevent my finally getting a shot in; but here is the whole adventure.

I lifted myself and looked over the edge into the next gulch. There was the ram, who saw me at the same moment, and rose. I probably missed him; for after my shot he continued to walk toward me in a leisurely manner, not fifty yards distant, I should think, down in his gulch. Whether I fired at him again or not, I *can't remember,*—couldn't remember that same evening when I tried to put the whole event faithfully down in my diary! Buck-fever is not the only reason for this uncertainty; for now, from behind every rock below me, horns rose up like tricks out of a trap-door, apparitions of horns everywhere, an invasion of mountain sheep. They came straight up to me,—this was the most upsetting part of it all. Not one did I see running down the gulch; they hadn't made me out, or made anything out, save that some noise had disturbed them. They came up and up around me, passing me, steadily coming and going on over the mountain while my buck-fever raged. "I saw their big grave eyes and the different shades of their hair, and noticed their hoofs moving—but whether they came by fast or slow, or what number there were, I cannot remember at all." Such are the actual words I wrote not more than six hours later, and I am glad to possess this searching record of that day and of my bygone state of mind; for with the best honesty in the world no man can from memory alone rebuild the minute edifice of truth that has been covered by the heap of fifteen gathering years. So I stood, crazy and inefficient, upon the mountains, and after a little no more sheep were there. A speck of conscious action remained with me, namely, that during the passage of the sheep I had held myself enough in control to get "a bead" on the broadside of two successively; I remembered following them along for a moment with my rifle before pulling the trigger. But these I never saw again, and know not where I hit them—if hit them I did. One trophy remains to show for this day. A ram that had been shot at some moment of the invasion returned to the gulch where I was, and stood at a short distance above me; and then I succeeded in placing one shot where I meant it to go.

The visions of this band, as it scattered in twos and threes after crossing my gulch, would incline me to guess there must have been from fifteen to twenty of them—all rams. Their sex is quite certain; the most intense impression that was given to my unstrung perceptions is of their huge curving horns and their solemn eyes. It is hateful to think that some of them were hurt and so went off to limp, or to die; and I am thankful to have but very few memories of wanton shooting, and some consoling ones of temptations resisted. These rams mostly escaped the indiscriminate blasts from my rifle; of this I am sure. I saw them, high and low, near and far, scuttling into safety over the steep ridges, or down into unseen cañons; and upon presently searching the vicinity, we found but one trace of blood. As for the buck-fever, it was the first seizure that I ever had, and it has proved the last. Why it should have held off in previous years and come down upon me in 1888, who shall say? You will wonder as much as I do that a silver-tip bear did not give me the slightest touch of it in July, 1887. A bear is more important game than a sheep; this grizzly was the first I had ever seen, and I was less experienced. Excitability is a matter of temperament that varies infinitely; but this scarcely explains why, with a bear to shoot, no cucumber could have been cooler than I was one year, and why the next, with these rams, I seem to have been a useless imbecile. The unexpected apparition of so many animals does not account for it, because when I raised myself to look over the ridge before my first shot that brought them into sight, I was shaking thoroughly.

These proceedings did not, at any rate, impair appetite. With the flavor of elk, deer, antelope, bear, and even porcupine, we were familiar; but wild mutton was still a great novelty, and we found it the most palatable of all. I say "we found it" and not "it was," because I have found a lump of dough sponged round a tin plate full of bacon grease so very delicious! The romance of wild game so mixes with its taste that we carve a venison steak with unction and respect. Yet I have come almost to think that our good old friend roast beef is more savory than anything we can find in the woods. If it is merely the pleasure of the table that you seek, take a good walk every day in the park, or even just up and down town, and the meats from your kitchen (if your lot is blest with a kitchen) will be superior to all the meats of camp. . . .

I had, one day in September, 1896, the singular good fortune to watch a mamma with her child for a period even longer than my observation of the ram at Livingston.

The Tetons lie just south of the Yellowstone Park, and directly upon the borders of Wyoming and Idaho. Any recent map might seem to prove this geography inaccurate, because, as I understand it, a late extension of the timber reservation reaches below these mountains, and most wisely includes both them and Jackson's Lake with the whole piece of country eastward to the Continental Divide. Of all places in the Rocky Mountains that I know, it is the most beautiful; and, as it lies too high for man to build and propser in, its trees and waters should be kept from man's irresponsible destruction; those forests feed the great river system of the Columbia and Snake. But I have been a poacher, according to the recent map. In 1896, however, the line was north of me by a few miles; and the day before I saw the ewe and the lamb, I had shot a ewe. It is, I believe, considered unsportsmanlike to do this: I have never seen the sportsman yet, though, who would not cheerfully bring home a ewe to an empty larder. Our larder was empty, even of fish, which had been plentiful until we had climbed up here among the Tetons, where the brooks ran too small for fish.

My object this second day was to find, if I could, a ram; and it proved one of those occasions (sadly rare in my experience) when, being disappointed of one's wish, something actually better descends from the gods, bringing consolation. It was a climb less severe than those of which I have already written, for our camp among the Tetons was close to the fourth story; less, I should suppose, than a thousand feet above our tent, the mountain grew bare of trees. Upward from this, it was not a long walk to snow.

When first I saw the mother and child, I already had them at a great disadvantage; they were, to be sure, where I had not expected them to be, but I was where they had not expected me to be; and thus I became aware of them a long distance below me, actually coming up to me by the trail I had come myself. Trail, you must understand, does not here mean a path beaten by men, or even by game, but simply the pleasantest way of getting up this part of the mountain. The mother had been taking her child upon a visit to the third story, had been away down among the pine woods and open places, where brooks ran and grass grew with several sorts of flowers and ripe berries; and now she was returning to the heights of her own especial world. Alas for my camera!

it was irretrievably in camp. I laid my useless rifle down, for from me neither of these lives should receive any hurt; and with the next best thing to a camera—my field-glasses—I got ready for a survey of this family as prolonged and thorough as they should allow. But field-glasses are a poor second best in such a case; a few pictures of this lady and her offspring "at home" would have told you more than my words have any hope of conveying.

I never saw people is less haste. From beginning to end they treated the whole mountain as you would treat your library (dining room were, perhaps, nearer the mark) upon an idle morning between regular meals. No well-to-do matron, with her day's housekeeping finished, could have looked out of the window more serenely than this ewe surveyed her neighborhood. The two had now arrived at what, in their opinion, was a suitable place for stopping. "Their" opinion is not correct; it was, I soon unmistakably made out, the mamma who—far more than the average American mother as American mothers go now—decided what was good and proper for her child. This lamb was being brought up as strictly as if it were English. They had just completed a somewhat long and unrelieved ascent,—so I had, at any rate, previously found it. This upper region of the mountain rose above the tree belt in three well-marked terraces which were rimmed by walls of rock extremely symmetrical. Each terrace made a platform fairly level and fairly wide, upon which one was glad to linger for a while before ascending the slant to the next terrace wall. I was seated at the edge of the top terrace, a floor of stones and grass and very thick little spruce and juniper bushes; the mamma had just attained the terrace next below me, and up the wall after her had climbed and scrambled the little lamb with (I was diverted to notice) almost as much difficulty as I had found at the spot myself. The mamma knew a good deal more about climbing than the lamb and I did.

There this couple stood in full view some few hundred feet—about three hundred, I should think—below me; and here sat I at my ease, like a person looking over a comfortable balcony, observing them through my glass. There was a certain mirth in the thought how different would have been the mamma's deportment had she become aware that herself, her child, and her privacy were all in the presence of a party who was taking notes. But she, throughout, never became aware of this, and I sat the witness of a domestic hour full of discipline, encouragement and instruction. The glasses brought them to a nearness not unlike peeping through the keyhole; I could see the color of their eyes. The lady's expression could easily have passed for critical. After throwing a glance round the terrace, her action to the lamb was fairly similar to remarking, "Yes, there are no improper persons here; you may play about if you wish."

Some such thing happened between them, for after waiting for the scrambling lamb to come up with her on the level and stand beside her, she appeared to dismiss it from her thoughts. She moved over the terrace, grazing a little, walking a little, stopping, enjoying the fine day, while her good child amused itself by itself. I feared but one thing,—that the wind might take to blowing capriciously, and give their noses warning that a heathen stranger was in the neighborhood. But the happy wind flowed gentle and changeless along the heights of the mountains. I have not more enjoyed anything in the open air than that sitting on the terrace watching those creatures whose innocent blood my hands were not going to shed.

After a proper period of relaxation, the mother judged it time to go on. There was nothing haphazard in her action; of that I am convinced. How she did it, how she intimated to the lamb that they couldn't stop here any longer, I don't pretend to know. I do, however, know that it was no mere wandering upward herself, confident the lamb would follow; because presently (as I shall describe) she quite definitely made the lamb stay behind. She now began mounting the hill right toward me, not fast but steadily, waiting now and then, precisely as other parents wait, for her toddling child to come up with her. Here and there were bushes of some close stiff leaf, that she walked through easily, but which were too many for the toddling child. The lamb would sometimes get into the middle of one of these and find itself unable to push through; after one or two little efforts, it would back out and go round some other way, and then I would see it making haste to where its mother stood waiting. Upon one of these occasions the mother received it with a manner that seemed almost to say: "Good gracious, at your age I found no trouble with a thing of that kind!" They drew, by degrees, so near me that I put away my glasses. There was a time when they were not fifty feet below me and I could hear their little steps; and once the ewe sneezed in the most natural manner. While I was wondering what on earth they would do when they found themselves stepping upon the terrace into my lap, the ewe saw a way she liked better. Had she gone to my left as I watched her, and so reached my level, the wind would have infallibly betrayed me; but she turned the other way and went along beneath the terrace wall to a patch of the bushes high enough to make severe work for the lamb. While she was doing this, I hastened to a new position. Where I had been sitting she was bound to see me as soon as she climbed twenty feet higher, and I accordingly sought a propitious cover, and found it in a clump of evergreens. She got to the wall where she could make one leap of it. It was done in a flash, and resembled nothing that any well-to-do matron could perform; but once at the top, she was again the complete matron. She scanned the new ground critically and with apparent satisfaction at first. I stole the glasses to my eyes and saw her closed lips wearing quite the bland expression of a lady's that I know when she has entered a room to make a call, and finds the wall-paper and furniture reflect, on the whole, favorably upon the lady of the house. Meanwhile, the poor little lamb was vainly springing at the wall; the jump was too high for it. Its front hoofs just grazed the edge, and back it would tumble to try again. Finally it bleated; but the mother deemed this not a moment for indulgence. She gave not the slightest attention to the cry for assistance. There was nothing dangerous about the place, no unreasonable hardship in getting the best of the wall; and by her own processes, whether you term them thought or instinct, she left her child to meet one of the natural difficulties of life, and so gain self-reliance.

Do you think this fanciful? That is because you have not sufficiently thought about such things. The mamma did undoubtedly not use the words "self-reliance" or "natural difficulties of life"; but if she had not her sheep equivalent for what these words import, her species would a long while ago have perished off the earth. The mountain sheep is a master at the art of self-preservation; its eye is tenfold keener than man's, because it has to be, and so is its foot ten or twenty fold more agile; every sense is developed to an extreme alertness. It measures foothold more justly than we do, because it has had to flee from dangers that do not beset us. That the maternal instinct (which these mothers retain until their young can shift for themselves) should fail in a matter so immediate as the needs of its young to understand rock climbing, is a notion more unreasonable than that it should be constantly attentive to this point. But—better than any talk of mine—the next step taken by the ewe will show how much she was climbing this mountain with an eye to her offspring.

The lamb had bleated and brought no sign from her. She continued standing, or moving a few feet onward in my direction. This means that she was coming up a quite gentle slant, and that thirty yards more would land her at my evergreen bush. She came nearer than thirty yards and abruptly stopped. She had suddenly not liked the looks of my evergreen. Behind her on one side, the last steep ascent of the mountain rose barer and barer of all growth to its stony, invisible summit which a curve of the final ridge hid from view. Behind her, down the quiet slant of the terrace, was the wall where she had left the lamb. She now backed a few stiff steps, keeping her eye upon the evergreen. Her uncertainty about it, and the ladylike reserve of her shut lips, caused me to choke with laughter. To catch a wild animal going through a (what we call) entirely human proceeding has always been to me a delightful experience; and from now to the end this sheep's course was as human as possible. I had been so engaged with watching her during the last few minutes that I had forgotten the lamb. The lamb had somehow got up the wall and was approaching. Its mamma now turned and moderately hastened down the slope to it. What was said between them I don't know; but the child came no farther in my suspicious direction; it stayed behind among some little bushes, and the mother returned to scrutinize my hiding-place. She looked straight at me, straight into my eyes it seemed, and her curiosity and indecision again choked me with laughter. She came even nearer than she had come before. How much of me she saw I cannot tell, but probably my hair and forehead; she at any rate concluded that this was no suitable place. She turned as I have seen ladies turn from a smoking-car, and with no haste sought her child again. How she managed their next move passes my comprehension; I imagined that every foot of the mountain ascent near me was in my full view. But it was not. Quite unexpectedly I now became aware of the two, trotting over the shoulder of the ridge above me, with already two or three times the distance between us that had been just now. If I had wished to follow them, it would have been useless, and I had seen enough. When I was ready, I made for the summit myself. The side which I had so far come up was the south side, and a little further climbing took me over the narrow shoulder to the north, where I was soon walking in long patches of snow. Across these in front of me went the tracks of the mamma and her lamb, the sage and gentle guide with the little novice who was learning the mountains and their dangers; across these patches I followed them for several miles, because my way happened to be theirs. No doubt they saw me sometimes; but I never saw them again. I hope no harm ever came to them; for I like to think of these two, these members of an innocent and charming race that we are making away with, as remaining unvexed by our noise and destruction, remaining serene in the freedom that lives among their pinnacles of solitude.

Preface to *Members of the Family*

In the preface to the first edition of The Virginian, *Wister discussed in objective terms the pastness of the West. Nine years later he was telling himself that "the happy hunting-ground of your young irresponsibility" had irrevocably passed, not only into history but into the personal past. In "The Mountain Sheep" he stood apart, superior in knowledge and expertise, from his younger self; here he attempts, knowing that it is impossible, to recover the freshness of his youthful feelings.*

The sources of those feelings are clearer to the mature Wister, but they are no less complex than they had been in "The White Goat." He associates the air of the West with a very European analogy, "the first five measures of Lohengrin." Although he pays homage to the great realists, he admits that his first fictional model was Prosper Merrimée's "Carmen." Although "Art is speaking aloud in grown-up company," he longs for the "Saturday eternal" of his early "nomadic, bachelor West." He is more hopeful about the artistic and political maturity of Americans and more wistful about his own circumstances.

Scipio LeMoyne, friend and supporter of the Virginian, appears in all but one of the stories in this volume as narrator, trickster central figure, or interlocutor and interpreter for the eastern narrator. He is the third version of Wister's western hero. Lin McLean had been with some difficulty converted into a romantic hero, and the Virginian was both the embodiment of "the last Cavalier" and the archetype of the superior human type who in all ages would rise to the top. In the stories in this volume, Wister almost seems relieved to have a central figure who, although shrewd and capable, has no long-term romantic or economic goals and who can speak to his "young irresponsibility."

Wister's desire to write more stories about the West was finally realized in the 1920s, when he completed the stories collected in When West Was West. *Compare, for example, the figure of the disgraced English nobleman in "The Evolution of the Cow-Puncher" and the central figure in "Right Honorable the Straw-berries." "At the Sign of the Last Chance" is consciously elegiac, not only for the author but for the characters.*

Wister notes in the Preface to the Collected Edition that the stories in Members of the Family *were written between 1900 and 1910, many of them after he had temporarily turned away from the West to write* Lady Baltimore *and the biographies of Grant and Washington.*

Source: Members of the Family *(New York: Macmillan, 1911). Part of the final paragraph has been deleted. The volume was illustrated by H. T. Dunn and was dedicated to Horace Howard Furness, whose son had, in 1891, challenged Wister to write about the West.*

WHEN THIS October comes, twenty years will be sped since the author of these Western tales sat down one evening to begin his first tale of the West, and will you forgive him a preamble of gossip, of retrospection? Time steps in between the now that is and the then that was with a vengeance; it blocks the way for us all; we cannot go back. When the old corner, the old place, the old house, wear the remembered look, beckon to the memory as if to say, No change here! then verily is the change worst, the shell most empty, the cheat well-nigh too piercing. In a certain garden I used to plunder in 1866, the smell to-day of warm, dusty strawber-ries. . . . But did we admit to our companionship ghosts only, what would living be? I continue to eat strawberries. As for smells, they're worse than old melodies, I think. Lately I was the sport of one. My train was trundling over the plains—a true train of the past, half freight, half passenger, cars of an obsolete build, big smoke-stack on the archaic engine, stops for meals, inveterate news-boy with bad candy, bad novels, bad bananas—a dear old horrible train, when magic was suddenly wrought. It came in through the open window, its wand touched me, and the evoked spirits rose. With closed eyes I saw them once more, standing there out in the alkali, the antelope by scores and hundreds, only a little way off, a sort of color between cinnamon and amber in the morning sun, transparent and phantom-like, with pale legs. Only a little way off. Eyes closed, I watched them, as in 1885 with open ones I beheld them first from the train. Now they were running; I saw the bobbing dots of their white receding rears, and through me passed the ghost of the first thrill at first seeing antelope yesterday—it seemed yesterday: only a little way off. I opened my eyes; there was the train as it ought to look, there were the plains, the alkali, the dry gullies, the mounds, the flats, the enormous sunlight, the virgin air like the first five measures of *Lohengrin*— but where were the antelope? So natural did everything continue to look, surely they must be just over that next rise! No; over the one beyond that? No; only a little, little way off, but gone for evermore! And magic smote me once again through the window. Thousands of cattle were there, with horsemen. Were they not there? Not over the next rise? No; gone for evermore. What was this magic that came in through the window? The smell of the sage-brush. After several years it was greeting me again. All day long it breathed a welcome and a sigh, as if the desert whispered: Yes, I look as if I were here; but I am a ghost, too, there's no coming back. All day long the whiffs of sage-brush conjured old sights before me, till my heart ran over with homesickness for what was no more, and the desert seemed to whisper: It's not I you're seeking, you're straining your eyes to see yourself,—you as you were in your early twenties with your illusion that I, the happy hunting-ground of your young irresponsibility, was going to be permanent. You must shut your eyes to see yourself and me and the antelope as we all used to be. Why, if Adam and Eve had evaded the angel and got back into the garden, do you think they would have found it the same after Cain and Abel? Thus moralized the desert, and I thought, How many things we have to shut our eyes to see!

Permanent! Living men, not very old yet, have seen the Indian on the war-path, the buffalo stopping the train, the cow-boy driving his cattle, the herder watching his sheep, the government irrigation dam, and the automobile—have seen every one of these slides which progress puts for a moment into its magic-lantern and removes to replace with a new one. The final tale in this book could not possibly have happened in the day of the first tale, although scarcely twenty years separate the new, present Wyoming from that cow-boy Wyoming which then flourished so boisterously, and is now like the antelope. Steam and electricity make short work of epochs. We don't know how many centuries the Indian and the buffalo enjoyed before the trapper and pioneer arrived. These latter had fifty or sixty good years of it, pushing westward until no west was left to push to; a little beyond Ogden in 1869, the driving of that golden spike which riveted the rails between New York and San Francisco, rang out the old, rang in the new, and progress began to work its magic-lantern faster. The soldier of the frontier, the frontier post—gone; the cattle-range—gone; the sheep episode just come, yet going already, or at any rate already mixed, diluted, with the farm, the truck garden, the poultry yard, the wife, the telephone, the summer boarder, and the Victor playing the latest Broadway "records" in valleys where the august wilderness reigned silent—yesterday. The nomadic, bachelor West is over, the housed, married West is established. This rush of change, this speed we live at everywhere (only faster in some places than in others) has led some one to remark sententiously that when a Western baby is born, it immediately makes its will, while when a New York baby is born, it merely applies for a divorce.

But what changes can ever efface that early vision which began with the antelope? Wyoming burst upon the tenderfoot resplendent, like all the story-books, like Cooper and Irving and Parkman come true again; here, actually going on, was that something which the boy runs away from school to find, that land safe and far from Monday morning, nine o'clock, and the spelling-book;

here was Saturday eternal, where you slept out-of-doors, hunted
big animals, rode a horse, roped steers, and wore deadly weapons.
Make no mistake: fire-arms were at times practical and imperative, but this was not the whole reason for sporting them on your
hip; you had escaped from civilization's schoolroom, an air never
breathed before filled your lungs, and you were become one large
shout of joy. College-boy, farm-boy, street-boy, this West melted
you all down to the same first principles. Were you seeking fortune? Perhaps, incidentally, but money was not the point; you had
escaped from school. This holiday was leavened by hard bodily
work, manly deeds, and deeds heroic, and beneath all the bright
brave ripple moved the ground-swell of tragedy. Something of
promise, also, was in the air, promise of a democracy which the
East had missed: —

"With no spread-eagle brag do I gather conviction each year
that we Americans, judged not hastily, are sound at heart, kind,
courageous, often of the truest delicacy, and always ultimately of
excellent good sense. With such belief, or, rather, knowledge, it is
sorrowful to see our fatal complacence, our as yet undisciplined
folly, in sending to our State Legislatures and to that general
business office of ours at Washington, a herd of mismanagers that
seems each year to grow more inefficient and contemptible,
whether branded Republican or Democrat. But I take heart,
because oftener and oftener I hear upon my journey the citizens
high and low muttering, 'There's too much politics in this country'; and we shake hands."

Such "insurgent" sentiments did I in 1895, some time before
insurgency's day, speak out in the preface to my first book of
Western tales; to-day my faith begins to be justified. In the West,
where the heart of our country has been this long while, and
where the head may be pretty soon, the citizens are awakening to
the fact that our first century of "self" government merely sub-
stituted the divine right of corporations for the divine right of
Kings. Surprising it is not, that a people whose genius for machinery has always been paramount should expect more from consti-
tutions and institutions than these mere mechanisms of government can of themselves perform; the initiative, referendum, and

recall are excellent inventions, but if left to run alone, as all our other patent devices have been, they will grind out nothing for us: By his very creed is the American dedicated to eternal vigilance. This we forgot for so long that learning it anew is both painful and slow. We have further to remember that prosperity is something of a curse in disguise; it is the poor governments in history that have always been the purest; where there is much to steal, there will be many to steal it. We must discern, too, the illusion of "natural rights," once an inspiration, now a shell from which life has passed on into new formulas. A "right" has no existence, save in its potential exercise; it does not proceed from within, it is permitted from without, and "natural rights" is a phrase empty of other meaning than to denote whatever primitive or acquired inclinations of man each individual is by common consent allowed to realize. These permissions have varied, and will vary, with the ages. Polygamy would be called a natural right now in some parts of the world; to the criminal and the diseased one wife will presently be forbidden in many places. Let this single illustration serve. No argument based upon the dogmatic premise of natural rights can end anywhere save in drifting fog. We see this whenever a meeting of anarchists leads a judge or an editor into the trap of attempting to define the "right" of free speech. In fact, all government, all liberty, reduces itself to one man saying to another: You may do *this;* but if you do *that,* I will kill you. This power Democracy vests in "the people," and our final lesson to learn is that in a Democracy there is no such separate thing as "the people"; all of us are the people. Truly this creed compels the American to eternal vigilance! Will he learn to live up to it?

From the West the tenderfoot took home with him the health he had sought, and an enthusiasm his friends fled from; what was Wyoming to them or they to Wyoming? In 1885 the Eastern notion of the West was "Alkali Ike" and smoking pistols. No kind of serious art had presented the frontier as yet. Fresh visits but served to deepen the tenderfoot's enthusiasm and whet his impatience that so much splendid indigenous material should literally be wasting its sweetness on the desert air. It is likely always to be true that in each hundred of mankind ninety-nine can see nothing new until the hundredth shakes it in their faces—and he must keep shaking it. No plan of shaking was yet in the tenderfoot's mind, he was dedicated to other calling; but he besieged the ears of our great painter and our great novelist. He told the painter of the strong, strange shapes of the buttes, the epic landscape, the color, the marvellous light, the red men blanketed, the white men in chapareros, the little bronze Indian children; particularly does he recall—in 1887 or 1888—an occasion about two o'clock in the morning in a certain beloved club in Boston, when he had been preaching to the painter. A lesser painter (he is long dead) sat by, unbelieving. No, he said, don't go. I'm sure it's crude, repulsive, no beauty. But John Sargent did believe. Other work waited him; his path lay elsewhere, he said, but he was sure the tenderfoot spoke truth. Other work awaited the novelist, too; both painter and novelist were wiser than to leave what they knew to be their own for unknown fields. But would no one then, disperse the Alkali Ikes and bring the West into American art and letters?

It was a happy day for the tenderfoot when he read the first sage-brush story by Mary Hallock Foote. At last a voice was lifted to honor the cattle country and not to libel it. Almost at the same moment Charles King opened for us the door upon frontier military life. He brought spirited army scenes to our ken, Mrs. Foote more generally clothed the civilian frontier with serious and tender art. They (so far as I knew) were the first that ever burst into that silent sea. Next, Mr. Roosevelt began to publish his vivid, robust accounts of Montana life. But words alone, no matter how skilfully used, were not of themselves adequate to present to the public a picture so strange and new. Another art was needed, and most luckily the man with the seeing eye and shaping hand arrived.

A monument to Frederic Remington will undoubtedly rise some day; the artist who more than any one has gathered up in a grand grasp an entire era of this country's history, and handed it down visible, living, picturesque, for coming generations to see— such man will have a monument. But in the manner of commemorating national benefactors, I would we resembled the French who celebrate their great ones—not soldiers and statesmen alone, but all their great ones—by naming public places in their honor: the Quai Voltaire, the Rue Bizet, the Rue Auber—to mention the first that come to memory. Everywhere in France you will meet with these instances of a good custom. In this country we seem to value even third-rate politicians more than first-rate men of art and letters. If Paris can by her streets perpetuate the memory of the composers of *Carmen* and *Fra Diavolo,* would it not be fitting that Denver, Cheyenne, Tucson, and other western cities, should have a Remington street? I am glad I did not wait until he was dead to pay my tribute to him. The two opportunities that came to me in his life I took, nor has my opinion of his work changed since then. If he never quite found himself in color, he was an incomparable draftsman; best of all, he was a great wholesome force making for independence, and he taught to our over-imitative American painters the needed lesson that their own country furnishes subjects as worthy as any that Delacroix or Millet ever saw. I have lived to see what I did not expect, the desert on canvas; for which I thank Fernand Lungren. Tributes to the dead seem late to me, and I shall take this chance to acknowledge my debt to some more of the living.

Four years after that night vigil with Sargent, the tenderfoot had still written no word about the West. It was in 1891, after repeated sojournings in camp, ranch, and military post, that his saturation with the whole thing ran over, so to speak, in the form of fiction. Writing had been a constant pastime since the school paper; in 1884 Mr. Howells (how kind he was!) had felt my literary pulse and pronounced it promising; a quickening came from the pages of Stevenson; a far stronger shove next from the genius of *Plain Tales from the Hills;* during an unusually long and broad wandering through the Platte valley, Powder River, Buffalo, Cheyenne, Fort Washakie, Jackson's Hole, and the Park, the final push happened to be given by Prosper Mérimée; I had the volume containing *Carmen* with me. After reading it in the Park I straightway invented a traveller's tale. This was written down after I got home—I left some good company at a club dinner table one night to go off to a lonely library and begin it. A second followed, both were sent to Franklin Square and accepted by Mr. Alden. Then I found my pretty faithfully-kept Western diaries (they would now fill a shelf) to be a reservoir of suggestion—and at times a source of despair; as, for instance, when I unearthed the following abbreviations: Be sure to remember Green-hides—perpendicular—sediment—Tuesdays as a rule.

Aware of Merimée's not highly expansive nature, I should hesitate, were he alive, to disclose my debt to his *Carmen*—my favorite of all short stories; but Mr. Howells and Mr. Kipling will be indulgent, and there is another who will have to bear with my gratitude. In 1896 I sat with him and he went over my first book, patiently, minutely pointing out many things. Everything that he said I could repeat this moment, and his own pages have continued to give me hints without end. That the pupil in one or two matters ventures to disagree with his benefactor may be from much lingering ignorance, or because no two ever think wholly alike: *tot homines quot sententia*, as the Latin grammar used so incontrovertibly to remark. It is significant to note how this master seems to be teaching a numerous young generation. Often do I pick up some popular magazine and read a story (one even of murder, it may be, in tropic seas or city slums) where some canny bit of foreshortening, of presentation, reveals the spreading influence, and I say, Ah, my friend, never would you have found out how to do that if Henry James hadn't set you thinking!

It can happen, says Montesquieu, that the individual through pursuing his own welfare contributes to the general good; Mr. Herbert Croly admirably and sagaciously applies this thought to the case of the artist and the writer. Their way to be worthy citizens and serve the State, he says, is to see to it that their work be reverently thorough, for thus they set high the standard of national excellence. To which I would add, that a writer can easily take himself too seriously, but he can never take his art too seriously. In our country, the painter and writer have far outstripped the working man in their ideal of honest work. This is (partly) because painter and writer have to turn out a good product to survive, while the working-man manages to survive with the least possible of personal effort and skill. Did I offer my publisher such work as the plumber and carpenter offer me, I should feel myself disgraced. Are we to see the day when the slovenly, lazy poet shall enact that the careful, industrious poet must work no longer and sell no more than he?

Editors have at times lamented to me that good work isn't distinguished from bad by our multifarious millions. I have the happiness to know the editors to be wrong. Let the subject of a piece of fiction contain a simple, broad appeal, and the better its art, the greater its success; although the noble army of readers will not suspect that their pleasure is largely due to the skill. Such a book as *The Egoist,* where the subject is rarefied and complex, of course no height of art will render acceptable, save to the rehearsed few. Thanks to certain of our more robust editors, the noble army grows daily more rehearsed, reads "harder" books than it did, accepts plainer speech and wider range of subject than the skittish spinster generation of a while ago. But mark here an underlying principle. The plain speech in Richardson was in his day nothing to start back from; to-day it is inhibited by a change in our circumambient reticence. The circumambient reticence varies in degree with each race, and almost with every generation of each race. Something like a natural law, it sets the limits for what can be said aloud in grown-up company—and Art is speaking aloud in grown-up company; it consists no more of the professional secrets of the doctor than it does of the prattle of the nursery. Its business is indeed to take notice of everything in life, but always subject to the circumambient reticence. Those gentlemen (and ladies) who utter that gaseous shibboleth about Art for Art (as well cry Beefsteak for Beefsteak) and would have our books and plays be foul because Ben Jonson frequently was and Anatole France frequently is, are out of their reckoning; and generally they may be suspected not so much of an abstract passion for truth as of a concrete letch for animalism. Almost the only advice for the beginner is, Clearly feel what you intend to express, and then go ahead, listening to nobody, unless to one who also perceives clearly your intention. Great and small things does this rule fit. Once in an early tale I sought to make our poor alphabet express the sound of cow-bells, and I wrote that they *tankled* on the hillside. In the margin I stated my spelling to be intentional. Back it came in the galley, tinkled. A revised proof being necessary, I restored my word with emphasis—and lo, tinkle was returned me again. I appealed to the veteran and well-loved sage at the head of *Harper's Magazine*. He supported me. Well, in the new Oxford dictionary, behold Tankle and me, two flies in amber, perpetuated by that Supreme Court; I have coined a new acknowledged word for the English language. This should not be told, but for its small moral, and if I could not render a final set of thanks to the living. Countless blunders have been saved me by the watchful eye of the printer and proofreader, those friends I never see, whose names I do not know. For twenty years they have marked places where through carelessness or fatigue I have slipped; may some of them know through this page that I appreciate their service.

This book is three years late; the first tale designed for it was published in 1901. Its follower should even now be ready. It is not yet begun; it exists merely in notes and intentions. Give me health and a day, sighs Emerson; and I am sorry for all who have to say that. When you see the new moon over your left shoulder, wish always for health; never mind all the other things. I own to an attachment for the members of this family; I would fain follow their lives a little more, into twentieth century Wyoming, which knows not the cow-boy and where the cow-boy feels at times more lost than ever he was on the range. Of all the ills that harass writing, plans deferred seem at times the worst; yet great pleasures offset them—the sight of one's pages in a foreign tongue, meeting horses in the Rocky Mountains named after the members of one's family, being asked from across the world for further news of some member. . . .

Old Yellowstone Days

Being offered a loan to get back on his feet must have been even more appealing to a man escaping from respectability than bathing naked below Niagara Falls, for it proved that he had thoroughly disguised himself. By this point, Wister had ceased either to condescend to or to mourn his early self or his companions, and had found a way of preserving a sense of them not just in formalized memory but in the living, lower depths of the mind. The final stream-of-consciousness passage, unique in Wister's writing, shows that he had not ceased to develop as a writer. And because it represents his deepest, freshest, and most characteristic response to the West, it serves as a fitting conclusion to his writing about it.

This essay includes passages from his diaries not reprinted in Owen Wister Out West.

Source: Harper's Monthly *172 (March 1936): 471–80.*

IN THE American we speak now they would have called us a bum bunch of guys. But this was 1887. I don't know what words those dusty tourists in the stagecoaches (whom we haughtily ignored) applied to us when we met them on the road; but we heard their sight-seeing screams, we saw them stare and crane their tame citified necks after us. Had we been bears or bandits (I am sure some of them took us for the latter) they couldn't have broken into more excitement. The bears in 1887 mostly kept themselves out of sight; they had a justifiable distrust of human nature, at least the black bears and silver-tips had; they had not yet learned that shooting in the Park was forbidden. But bandits you might see—possibly; there have been hold-ups in the Park. And there is no doubt that the Park with its violent phenomena could throw some visitors into a very special state of mind; they became ready to expect anything, they were credulous to the point of distortion.

We were merely five white men and one Indian, on six horses, with eight packs, in single file, riding at a walk, perfectly harmless, and as new to the Park as were the tourists who leaped from the stagecoaches to snapshot us. Variously scattered among these United States, our cavalcade may still be enshrined in albums of photographic souvenirs. Of course we were not the sort of spectacle you are likely to see, unless the circus or rodeo comes to town. At the cañon, a well-to-do youth whose acquaintance I had made the year before at Jackson in the White Mountains, recognized me, came up, shook my hand with solicitude, and said that if a hundred dollars would help. . . . And they put us all safe and far at a side table at the Mammoth Springs, so as not to alarm the tourists. I find in my diary that my spurs jingled so boisterously upon the wooden floors in that hotel that I removed them, blushing the while.

My diary reveals to me that I had forgotten more than I recollected of that first camping trip; so novel, so vivid, so charged with adventure and delight and lusty vigor and laughter, that to think of it makes me homesick for the past—and the past comes to be the mental home of those who can look back a long way. Weeks before we had excited the tourists, or washed our underwear in a geyser, other experiences had marked that summer as a high spot among holidays. George and I had swum naked in the quiet edge of the whirlpool below Niagara Falls; we had ridden on the cowcatcher all through the mountain-scenery of the Canadian Pacific (you couldn't do that now, the cowcatcher is shrunk to a mere shadow of its former self, but it's the best seat in the train for a view). We had seen Seattle as a ragged village of one lumpy street and frame houses, reached by steamers alone; a short railroad with a long title—Seattle Lake Shore and Eastern—carried lumber only, and soon terminated at a place called by humorists (I must suppose) Stuck Junction. The University, into which I wandered through a wooden gate swung shut by a chain weighted by a tin can filled with stones, matched its large name as imperfectly as the railroad. In an upper room I found a blackboard and a stuffed owl; and in this company sat a lone young woman reading *Les Misérables*. She asked me what the word in queer letters on a front page meant; and I could tell her, because Greek was required when I entered Harvard. Presently followed seven glorious days and nights in San Francisco, the High Jinks of the Bohemian Club among the great redwoods—but I am meandering; I must get back to the one red man and the five whites and the Park.

The red man was Tighee, a full-blooded Shoshone, speaking English incompletely, and seldom speaking at all. He was our huntsman. Two of the whites were cook, packer and horse wrangler; we were the other three; and in my pocket I carried a letter from General Sheridan, recommending me to all officers of the Army. Thirty-six hours in the stage from Rawlins on the railroad to Fort Washakie on the Shoshone Indian reservation brought us to our point for outfitting. Once outfitted, we started northwestward, and reached Wind River the second day. And here goes my diary:

"This afternoon George saw about six wild geese waddling about in a stream. He was desirous to test his horse's taste for shooting, so he fired from the saddle, thereby adding one to the number of geese. Nobody hurt." I had forgotten this.

It was the Sheridan Trail we followed up Wind River. Four years before us, General Sheridan, with President Arthur and a large escort, had taken this same route. It was nothing but a trail; solitary, wild, the Divide to our left, buttes and sagebrush to our right, and the streaming river beside us. Up the river 90 miles or so, and over a low part of the Continental Divide a bit south of Two-gwo-tee Pass, and down the Gros Ventre into Jackson's Hole, after lingering and killing bear and elk on the Divide. (It was curious to ride by, in 1893, the site of that camp two miles down the Pacific side from the summit of the Divide, that place which had been our headquarters for ten days, and find the stakes we had stretched our bear hides on in 1887 still in the ground, not one missing.)

Again my diary: "Sunday, Aug. 21. Camp 10. Head of Jackson's Lake, 7 p.m. Got here last night after 32 or 33 more miles . . . The Tetons across the lake magnificent. I hunted all day for elk with Tighee—9 till 4—in cross timber. Awful. Tracks everywhere. Only 2 elk—which I missed like a fool. Our friend the horse thief joined us yesterday. He turned out a harmless shepherd with a nice dog, who eats your supper when we are not looking."

Of course I had forgotten about missing the elk; any thoughtful man would. But why forget the dog?

And here let me pause to lay my ineffectual but heartfelt curse upon the commercial vandals who desecrated the outlet of Jackson's Lake with an ugly dam to irrigate some desert land away off in Idaho. As that lake used to be, it narrowed in a long bend by degrees, until placidly and imperceptibly it became once more the Snake River sliding out of it below as the Snake River had flowed into it above. Serenity and solitude everywhere; antelope in herds like cattle in the open spread of sagebrush between Snake and the Tetons; these rising from the dusky blur of pines to steeps of grass, slants of rock, streaks of snow like linen drying away up, and at last the far peaks. At sunset they turned lilac, and all their angles swam together in a misty blue. Just below the outlet among scattered pines near the river, an old cabin, gaping to the weather, roof going, each year a little less of a shelter, made the silence seem more silent, the past more distant, the wilderness more present. And there among the brush was a tattered legend in print: "This very fine old rum is widely known." This relic of man crashed into the quiet spell of nature not nearly so harshly as does that disgusting dam. There is more beauty in Jackson's Hole than even such a beastly thing could kill; but it has destroyed the august serenity of the lake's outlet for ever; and it has defaced and degraded the shores of the lake where once the pines grew green and dark. They stand now white skeletons, drowned by the rising level of the water.

The Sheridan trail left the lake and the river and crossed three miles of level, turned up into timber, ran through a valley of young symmetric spruce like a nursery; cold air came up to us from a stream flowing invisible in the depths of a little cañon; and by and by we descended to a flat of thick willows that brushed your knees as the trail sneaked through them till you came out on Snake again, forded it, and met discipline and law at the sergeant's cabin. Our packs were proud with trophies, heads and pelts; lucky that we needed no more of these to justify our wild and predatory aspect and prove our competence with the rifle; for here we crossed the sacred line, the southern boundary (as it was then) of the Park; and all shooting must cease; we had entered the sanctuary. The sergeant sealed our rifles. We took our way into the haunted land, the domain possessed of devils, shunned by the Indians of old.

II

Strange how readily the American mind swallows whole the promises in a political platform, and believes so little in any other statements, unless it is those of quack medicines! Vesuvius and Aetna had been heard of in the United States, long before John Colter of the Lewis and Clark expedition came back from his wild explorations and told the people of St. Louis about the hissing and rumbling and boiling phenomena he had beheld during his wanderings in the region of the upper Yellowstone. They set him down for a liar, and as a liar he passed for a matter of fifty years. During these, James Bridger got the same reputation. There's not a doubt that other white men saw the wonders of that weird country during those fifty years. Their traces have been found. But they were Hudson Bay fur trappers, and because of the fur they kept the secret. Not until gold-seekers rushed into Montana and parties of them (in 1863) actually saw much more of the wonders than even Colter had, were his words substantiated—or they might have been had gold not so utterly obsessed the minds of these prospectors that they hardly noticed the geysers. It was in 1870, through the official reports of a special expedition, that the whole country knew and believed for the first time that the hissing and boiling, with many other strange things, were no myth—

realized this too soon for vandal exploiters, like the builders of the Jackson Lake dam, to grab and spoil; for the Government took charge of the place and by law set it aside for the recreation of the people.

As we rode into it from the sergeant's cabin through jack pines and fallen timber, at a walk, "haunted" did not seem a far-fetched expression. Mud spots of odd hue and consistency were passed; one's horse went down into them deep and suddenly; once through the trees we saw a little pond steaming; stealthy, unusual smells prowled among the pines; after skirting Lewis Lake, the trail diverged from where the present road runs north across the Divide to the Thumb, and after going northwest along Shoshone Lake, went over the Divide at a rockier place, and so down the Fire Hole River through the trees toward the geysers; and my diary says:

"The Basin came in sight over the tree-tops below us—merely a litter of steam-jets. It might have been Lowell." Yes; the prospect suggested to my modern mind a manufacturing center in full swing. No wonder those shooting columns of steam scared the Indians of old.

The hotel at the Upper Geyser Basin was chiefly of canvas, walls and roof; and to sleep there must have made you intimately acquainted with how your neighbors were passing the night. We didn't sleep there, we camped within the trees a short ride away; but we rejoiced in the blackberry brandy we bought from the hotel clerk; it was provided to check disturbances which drinking queer water from highly chemical brooks often raised in human interiors. And we also rejoiced in a bath the soldiers had constructed in a cabin by the river. The cool river flowed into the wooden trough one way and through another spout, which you let loose with a wooden peg, astonishingly hot water poured from a little boiling hole in the formation above the cabin, and brought your bath to the temperature you desired. Both brandy and bath were a source of rejoicing; and after emerging clean and new from the latter, the spectacle of a little gray bird, like a fat catbird, skimming along the river like a bullet and suddenly dropping below the surface where it was shallow, and walking along the bottom with its tail sticking out in the air, filled me with such elation that I forgot the geysers and watched him. Where it was deeper he would plunge wholly out of sight, run along submerged, reach a shallow place, with his tail again sticking out. Then he would take it into his head to float on top and swim. I came to know him well. In 1896 I took his photograph high among the Teton range. I was washing at the creek before breakfast. He was sitting on a stone covered with snow in the middle of the creek, singing blithely; the water ouzel.

But I do not think that anybody there rejoiced quite as utterly as a boy employed in the hotel. He must have been somewhere in his 'teens; he was like the true love in "Twelfth Night" that could sing both high and low. In calm moments he would answer you in a deep bass. In excitement, into which he periodically fell, the bass cracked to a wild treble. He would be called a bell-hop to-day; in that day no bell was there, but the boy hopped a good deal. We would be sitting tilted back, reading our mail, the tourists would have ceased talking and be lounging drowsily, the boy would be at the door, motionless as a set steel trap. Suddenly the trap would spring, the boy would catapult into the door, and in his piping treble scream out:

"Beehive's a-goin' off!"

at which every tourist instantly started from his chair, and a leaping crowd gushed out of the hotel and sprinted down over the formation to catch the Beehive at it. Beehive finally quiescent, they returned slowly, sank into chairs and exhausted silence; you could have heard a mosquito. But the steel trap was again set, sprang soon, and again the silence was pierced:

"There goes Old Faithful!"

Up and out they flew once more, watched Old Faithful, and came back to their chairs and to silence more exhausted.

Was the boy exhausted? Never. It might be the Castle, it might be the Grotto—whatever it might be, that pre-Ritz-Carlton bell-hop routed those torpid tourists from their repose to set them trooping across the formation to gape at some geyser in action, and again seek their chairs, feebler each time. Has he in his mature years ever known more joy? I doubt it.

An Englishman, who sat with me (it may have been that year or a later one) on the hotel's narrow porch, had evidently had his credulity so distorted by the freaks of nature he had seen that everything amazed him. Had I seen any gray geese? Yes, I had. But large flocks? Well, I didn't know.

"There are large flocks of them, sir. Gray geese. Large flocks. God bless my soul! I saw them yesterday."

And just about then, Old Faithful played.

"How high do you take that column of water to be?"

I told him the number of feet I had been told.

"Dear me, no. You must be wrong. I understand that ridge over there is the Continental Divide?"

I believed it was.

"Well, sir, are you aware that the Continental Divide is some six thousand-and-odd feet high, and that geyser is rising into the sky clear above that ridge?"

My diary: "Friday, August 26. Washing clothes at a small geyser. . . . We steep the garment in a quiet blue pool, deep, and shaped exactly like a great calla lily, filled to the brim and some ten feet across. Then we soap and then with a pole poke it down a spluttering crevice that foams all over it until it is ready to take out and dry."

Have you ever soaped a geyser? Then you know it is true. If you have not you may think I am taking advantage of your credulity. Science explains the matter; I need not. But to soap a geyser is very bad for it; disturbs its rhythm, dislocates its circulation, makes it play when it isn't due to play, has killed one important geyser, I have heard. Before 1887, and before the effect of soap on geysers was widely known, a Chinaman had set up a laundry above an unemployed and inconspicuous vent in the formation at the Upper Geyser Basin. Hot water boiled in the vent, steam rose from it day and night, and the Chinaman was happy in the thought of needing neither fire nor stove nor pots, since he had taken Mother Nature into partnership, and she would wash his linen with her own hands. A few seconds after the first bundle of soaped clothes was stirred into the vent out jumped the geyser, hissing and spitting, and away blew the roof. The Chinaman escaped. That is the story; and early in my western adventures, when what they were telling me grew very remarkable, I always said, "Let me assure you that I make it a rule to believe everything I hear." But when they told me of a hole into which you could toss your soiled handkerchief and have it disappear and in a minute be thrown out washed, ironed, folded, and with a laundry mark, I drew the line. That Chinaman in 1887 had an establishment behind the hotel, where I saw the huge unnatural cucumbers he had raised with the help of hot moisture from the bowels of the earth; but his laundry was now beside, not above, Mother Nature's boiling water. By the time I had camped several times through the Park the uncertain temper of these bubbling holes had been more generally rumored. Not far from the Mud Geyser one day, I was passing a little girl who was poking one of them about the size of a soup plate with a stick, when a loud voice, which I presume was her mother's, shouted behind me:

"Louisa, quit fooling with that thing or it'll bust!"

Why will people scrawl their silly names on the scenery? Why thus disclose to thousands who will read this evidence that you are a *thoughtless ass?* All very well if you wrote your name, your address, and the date on the North Pole; but why do it in some wholly accessible spot where your presence represents no daring, no endurance, nothing but the necessary cash to go there? Around the base of Old Faithful (for example) are little scoops in the formation, little shallow white saucers into which the hot water has flowed and remained. Well, beneath the water on the bottom of these saucers the names of asses were to be seen, written in pencil. I doubt if this often happens nowadays; it doesn't pay. It was a deep satisfaction to talk of the vandals with Major Harris, or Captain Boutelle, or George Anderson, or Jack Pitcher, military commandants of the Park before it was turned over to the Department of the Interior. The opinions they variously expressed about those who defaced nature were to the point. And they devised punishment for the offenders before punishment was provided by law. The soldiers patrolled the places where vandalism was likely to occur. If they caught a tourist writing on the formation or breaking it off they stopped him, compelled him to efface the writing and give up the specimen. If they found a name after its writer had gone on they rode after him and brought him back to rub it out. It has happened that a man, having completed the round of the Park, has been about to take the train when his name, discovered on the formation by a soldier and telephoned to the Mammoth Springs, has led to its being duly and fittingly effaced by himself, escorted back clean across the Park. Captain Edwards (not a commandant, but on duty there in 1891) told me this:

A soldier at the Upper Basin had reported a clergyman as having broken off a bagful of formation. Edwards found him seated in the stage, about to depart from the Fountain.

"You have taken no specimens of course?"

"No."

"You give me your word as a preacher of the Gospel that you have nothing of the sort in that bag?"

"I do."

Edwards let him go.

"But why?" I asked.

"I couldn't humiliate a minister in front of the crowd."

Boutelle had a hard time to stop a commercial clique from installing an elevator at the Lower Falls. Politics was behind it, as usual. To put a lot of machinery by those Falls at the head of that cañon, where the sublime merges with the exquisite, and which alone is worth crossing the continent to see, would have been an outrage more abominable than the dam at Jackson Lake.

"But why should your refined taste," objected a lover of the multitude to whom I told this, "interfere with the enjoyment of the plain people?"

"Have the plain people told you or anybody that the one thing they lie sleepless craving for is an elevator to go up and down by those falls the way they do in hotels?"

"They would like it if it was there."

"Of course they would. Is that a reason to vulgarize a supreme piece of wild natural beauty for all time? How are the plain people to learn better things than they know if you lower to their level everything about it?"

But who could convince a female philanthropist?

The would-be exploiter of the Park never dies. It may be a railroad, a light and power company—anything. It is a ceaseless menace, invariably supported by plausible argument and political influence. Had the language of the original act setting the Park aside in 1872 for the benefit and enjoyment of the people been so phrased as to bar exploiters as it was phrased to protect the game and fish from capture or destruction "for the purposes of merchandise and profit," safety from the despoiler would be better assured. Boutelle staved off the exploitation during his term as commandant. But George Anderson related many tales of poachers and attempted exploitation. None of them was quite so evil as they way the army canteen was abolished; but as that concerns not the Park, but the enlisted man, and a clique of distillers, and the Federated Spinsters of Uplift, it does not belong here; I doubt if it is ever told.

My diary: "Monday, August 29. West, George Norman, and I are having a hell of a time trying to get down to the bottom of the cañon with ropes. . . . I am at present sitting about nowhere, halfway . . . George is above, undecided whether he'll untie the rope from the last tree, or not."

As I read this over—it was written forty-nine years ago—West's remarks at various stages of our descent come back to me: (1) that he would give ten dollars not to have started, (2) that he would give fifty, (3) that he hadn't enough cash in the world to give what he'd like to. We got all the way down and back without hurt. It was somewhere between Inspiration Point and the Falls. Farther down there's no trouble, there's a trail to the water, where you can catch trout.

III

When we returned to the Park in 1896 many changes had occurred in it since our first sight of it in 1887. The stage road now went from the Upper Basin to the Thumb, no longer (as we had gone then) from the Lower Basin up Nez Percé Creek and over the Divide by Mary's Mountain along Trout Creek in the Hayden Valley to the Yellowstone River between the Mud Geyser and the

Sulphur Mountain. There you met the road between the Cañon and the Thumb; and the hotel at the Cañon could easily have been dropped whole into the great reception room of the present hotel there. Its site was not at all the same—it was about at the junction of the road to Norris; it had but one storey, and its shape reminded you of a bowling alley or a shooting gallery.

We didn't go to the Lake in 1887. I have often seen it since, and once camped and fished at the outlet for a number of days. Not much to record of that, except the occasional wormy trout—you know them by their feeble fight, their unwholesome color, and their emaciation (I believe their state is due to a parasite peculiar to the waters of the Yellowstone Lake, I never caught any elsewhere than in the Lake or the river below it) and the reprehensible conduct of the sea gulls one day: that is unforgettable. I was catching many fish and cleaning them, and the cleanings attracted some dozen gulls. They hovered in the air, swooped on the guts I cut out of each trout, gobbled them and were ready for more. There was a young gull among them, and he was never quick enough for his parents, or his uncles, or his aunts. They always got there first, sometimes only a second ahead of him, snapped it from under his callow beak, and left him sadder and sadder. At length in pity I threw a large meal close to him; he got it, made off along the shore by himself a little way, and had it partially swallowed, when an adult relative spied it, dashed down, dragged it out of his poor little throat, and it was gone. He acted precisely like a child of three in a parlor car. He threw his head up to the sky, beat his wings, shut his eyes, opened his beak, and bawled and bawled.

Long before 1896 the hotels were larger, and the education of the bears had begun. They were now aware that man did not shoot them and they had discovered that campers carried good things to eat. One night in 1891 our sleep was murdered by sudden loud rattling and clashing of our tin plates and other hardware. We rushed out of the tent into silence and darkness. In the morning our sugar sack lay wounded, but still with us. Macbeth while dragging at it had tumbled the hardware about him. He was not educated enough to stand that and had taken to the woods. Another bear took to a tree that week. As dusk was descending, campers found him in suspicious proximity to their provender and raised a shout. The shouting brought us and others not to the rescue, but to the highly entertaining spectacle of a tree surrounded by fascinated people waving their arms, and a bear sitting philosophically above their din. Night came on, the campers went to bed, and the bear went away. Many years have now gone since the bears discovered the treasures that are concealed in the garbage piles behind the hotels. I walked out once in the early evening at the Lake hotel and counted twenty-one bears feasting. I saw a bear march up to a tourist and accept candy from his hand, while his wife, stood at a safe distance, protesting vainly, but I think rightly. I saw the twenty-one bears suddenly cease feasting and withdraw to a short distance. Out of the trees came a true grizzly, long-snouted and ugly; and while he selected his dinner with ostentatious care and began to enjoy it, a cinnamon bear stole discreetly, as if on tip-toe, toward the meal he had left behind him. He got pretty near it, when the grizzly paused in eating and merely swung his head at him—no more than that; in a flash the cinnamon had galloped humpty-dumptily off and sat down watching. He came back presently; and the scene was re-enacted three times before I had enough of it and left; each time when the cinnamon had reached a certain point the grizzly swung his head, and this invariably sufficed. It is my notion that the cinnamon was a bit of a wag.

As our outfit rode into the Mammoth Springs, Tighee at sight of the hotel made (I think) his first remark that day:

"All same one big mountain."

What would he have said to the present hotel? It dwarfs the old one, which is where the stage-drivers and various employees live—or did on my last visit there in 1916. What would he have said about the Old Faithful Inn, which has long replaced that primitive canvas affair where the blackberry brandy and the bell-hop once flourished, and the Englishman had been amazed at the gigantic height of Old Faithful in action, and the flocks of gray geese? These birds have amazed me, but not in the same way. Dawn after dawn in camp above Crawford's shack by Jackson Lake, two of us left warm beds for the freezing air, and crawled like turtles towards a flat where the geese were feeding. We sneaked along, so close to the cold earth that the brush hid the geese from us. Every day the flock saw us first, flapped up far out of range, and departed. I am certain that they had a sentinel posted and enjoyed us as the cinnamon did the grizzly.

"To call these birds geese," I said to my companion, "is an outrage."

"Or rather," he corrected me, "the term is misapplied to foolish persons."

What do you think of that?

Upon another occasion, while at breakfast, I contemplated a pot of preserves made in Dundee, and remarked:

"Who could have expected orange marmalade to come from Scotland?"

And he explained: "They import the oranges, you know."

Eight weeks of that. It came near to aging me.

Something worse—no, almost as bad—happened during those same eight weeks. I cannot tell if Tighee would have treated us so had we taken him away from the beaten track. We never did, in the Park or out of it; for though we had hunted and fished in a virtually untenanted wilderness, the Sheridan Trail ran through it, familiar ground to Tighee; and in the Park we followed the conventional route and visited none except the regulation sights. But with Dick Washakie (our hunter on this later excursion, another full-blooded Shoshone, who spoke a little more English, having once been at the Carlisle school) we struck off the beaten trail. I was anxious to get mountain sheep after visiting the geysers and Cañon; so I turned our backs on the known and our faces to the unknown, using maps, and no longer consulting Dick Washakie about where we should go next. I wished if it were possible to get into the high country eastward, where three ranges of mountains may be said to collide and produce steep and complicated results, far from tourists, far from everybody. The third morning—we were nowhere near the high country yet—West came and told me Dick Washakie was leaving us. So I went to him. His horse was packed. Nothing availed. Not our predicament, not the wages he would lose, nothing. He gave so many reasons—his father was old—he must cut his hay—I forget the rest—that I knew he never gave the real one.

A previous experience with another Indian, Paul La Rose, made me certain that West had guessed right: they distrusted country where they had never been. With Paul La Rose we had forded Snake below the outlet. He objected to fording it at all. At every step we took on the far side he objected more. I kept on. From the Sheridan trail on the east side of Snake. I had stared too many days across the spread of land at the Tetons; I intended to get close to them. We should find no water, said Paul. Look at the snow up there, I said; that must melt and feed some creek at the base of those big mountains. We'd better turn back, said Paul. We'll go on, Paul. Well, you'll have dry camp to-night. Paul, we'll go on. You take the lead then. He dropped sulkily away from the head of our procession, I took his place, and in about an hour we heard the quiet sound of a waterfall and came to an opening in the narrow belt of pines to which I headed, and found the stream that flows between Leigh's and Jenny's Lake. At that camp we fished and hunted for a week in solitude unbroken. That was 1888. Since then the dude ranch has been established in that country, Snake is bridged.

But Dick Washakie's desertion changed our plans; we needed a hunter. We renounced that high country where the mountain ranges collide and journeyed back into the known; and so began my acquaintance with Yancey. Yancey was of that frontier type which is no more to be seen; the goat-bearded, shrewd-eyed, lank Uncle Sam type. He and his cabins had been there a long while. The legend ran that he was once a Confederate soldier, and had struck out from the land of the Lost Cause quite unreconstructed, and would never wear blue jeans because blue reminded him of the Union army. He was known as Uncle John by that whole country. One of his cabins was a rough wayside inn for miners traveling between Cinnabar and Cooke City at the northeastern edge of the Park. Yancey did not talk much to mere people; and I should have been mere people to him, but that I knew Boies Penrose (later Senator from Pennsylvania), who had camped more than once on Hell Roaring Creek nearby, and for whose good shooting, fishing, and horsemanship the old timer had warm respect. He unbent at the name of Penrose. What could he do for me? I told him of our hunterless plight. James Woody was due to-morrow. He would guide us to a sheep country. And then Uncle John led me across the road to—not his wine, but his whisky cellar. Handsome barrels. I came to know it well. He had some sort of fermented stuff made from oranges, which he obtained from California. Mingled properly with whisky, the like of it I have never elsewhere tasted. Woody didn't want to go. He was waiting to join Theodore Roosevelt; but on Yancey's persuasion he would go with us, leave us where sheep were to be expected, and send Donohue in his stead. I had no money for wages here; it was in a safe at Fort Washakie, where I had expected to pay Dick off. I wrote East and, just like a play, an old Cinnabar acquaintance of 1887 turned up and was glad to convey the letter to the mail. Joe Keeney was his name, and we became acquainted thus:

My diary, Sept. 1: "A lucky chance made us cared for at Cinnabar. When were were some 500 yards from it (it is merely a railroad depot, one saloon, a hotel, and some sheds) a little child passed us full tilt. As there was a ranch behind us we did not stop her, but supposed she was going there. Then far ahead we saw a man beckoning violently. When we came to him he said, 'Damn it, I signalled to head her off.' 'Well, I didn't see you. Get on my horse and go after her.' Which he did, catching her and bringing her back in his arms. It appeared he had sent her with a message to some men in a buggy who were stopping at the ranch but started away before she could get to them. 'And she'd have run till she ran them down in the mountains,' her parent added. He turned out to be the landlord, Joe Keeney, who became our friend, gave us drinks, and turned his family out of their room and made us sleep in it."

Joe Keeney rode off from Yancey's with my letter under his hat, so as not to forget it; James Woody guided us to the Hoodoos (which are pillared erosions of sandstone, and look like a church organ that has met with a railroad accident); Donohue arrived in his place and took us to Saddle Mountain; I got a black tail, but never a sheep, nothing of interest save petrified fragments of wood and seashells lying over a region at present six or seven thousand feet above sea level; we returned to Yancey's where a letter was put in my hand. It was muddy. It was my own. Joe Keeney must have scratched his head on the way to Gardner (to which the railroad had now been extended from Cinnabar). I was penniless. As I lay in camp in the meadows toward Baronet's bridge next morning, Yancey came by.

"What can I do for you?"

"Whisky and that orange shrub. And lend me a hundred dollars."

He did.

Back home, I sent him a flask engraved "John Yancey, from the Dead Beat," with the date.

He was at Livingston the next autumn when I stopped off with the skins of white goat I had shot in the mountains of Washington territory. Those skins increased his respect for me; we went to a show that evening, and through the night I was introduced, I think, to the whole town, male and female.

In these days, the Park bear has almost completed his education. His children for generations have known the way to the garbage pile. And all have learned the hour when the train of stages passes along the road through the various woods. Along the road they wait, begging; and the tourists place chocolate and other dainties in their paws and maws. They have gone on the dole. The one step remaining is for them to take charge of the hotels and expel the management.

Yancey is gone, Beaver Dick is gone; awake at night sometimes, the tide of streamline thought sets West, and I recall that porcupine tastes like roast pig it was a hornets' nest in that tree across the trail the pack horse trod into and the dutch oven fell off first and he bounced down through the timber with the tin plates rolling every which way the roll of bedding stuck in a bush but you get tired of trout we caught little minnows thick as mosquitoes in a net in that camp above Jenny's Lake for white bait I shouldn't want to see Brook's Lake now any fool can go along the road in a car and find his way there just below was where we clubbed those young geese they couldn't fly yet swimming Wind River was just a creek very good tender eating so was the sand hill crane Copley Amory short but not like the young geese the white columbine at that camp larger than the garden sort and there was a white swan out on the lake gosh how good it used to be to swab up the melted lard off your tin plate with a lump of bread and swallow it was it wild carrots or parsnips that would poison gosh those miles of flowers in the big meadow below the scoop in the rocks where Grant La Farge found we could get out and cross the Divide . . . and so on, and so on.

Works Cited and Bibliography

PRIMARY BIBLIOGRAPHY

Sherman, Dean. "Owen Wister: An Annotated Bibliography," *Bulletin of Bibliography* 28 (January–March 1971): 7–16. Not definitive, but the fullest listing available.

SECONDARY BIBLIOGRAPHY

Marovitz, Sanford E. "Owen Wister: An Annotated Bibliography of Secondary Material," *American Literary Realism* 7 (Winter 1974): 1–110.
Arranged by year; author index; summary annotations of all items.

PRIMARY MATERIALS

Owen Wister Out West: His Journals and Letters, edited by Fanny Kemble Wister. Chicago: University of Chicago Press, 1958.
A selection of Wister's diaries, 1885–95, from his first trip west to the confirmation of his career as a professional writer. Letters to Wister's mother and others as well as comments by the editor (his daughter) are interpolated. Indispensable.

That I May Tell You: Journals and Letters of the Owen Wister Family, edited by Fanny Kemble Wister. Wayne, Penn.: Haverford House, 1979.
Contains "The Early Years of a Child of Promise," by Wister's mother, Sarah, the fullest account of Wister's boyhood and early manhood, including his decision to give up music. Also prints letters between Owen and Molly Wister and the editor's reminiscences of her childhood.

Wister, Owen. *Roosevelt: The Story of a Friendship: 1880–1919*. New York: Macmillan, 1930.
Contains a good deal of autobiographical material, though corrections from later documents are often necessary.

SECONDARY MATERIALS

Cobbs, John L. *Owen Wister*. Boston: Twayne Publishers, 1984.
Consciously introductory but useful within its modest limits. Mistakes the title of "The Evolution of the Cow-Puncher," which may indicate further flaws.

Payne, Darwin. *Owen Wister: Chronicler of the West, Gentleman of the East*. Dallas: Southern Methodist University Press, 1985.
Based on the first thorough investigation of the Wister papers. Better at giving the texture of Wister's life than at interpreting it or placing it in larger contexts.

Vorpahl, Ben Merchant. *My Dear Wister: The Frederic Remington-Owen Wister Letters*. Palo Alto: American West Publishing Company, 1972.
Reprints letters and other materials by the two principals, places them into a context, and interprets them. Essential.

Watkins, George Thomas III. "Owen Wister and the American West: A Biographical and Critical Study." Ph.D. dissertation, University of Illinois, 1959.
Particularly good on the cattle business, geography, and society as Wister found it during his early trips west. Watkins's textual studies of various versions of stories and novels are also valuable. His critical judgments, heavily Jamesian, are perhaps less useful.

White, G. Edward. *The Eastern Establishment and the Western Experience: The West of Frederic Remington, Theodore Roosevelt, and Owen Wister*. New Haven: Yale University Press, 1968.
A major study in cultural and literary history essential to students of Wister and of the whole period.